AMERICAN WORDS

American Words

by

MITFORD M. MATHEWS

ILLUSTRATED BY *Lorence Bjorklund*

THE WORLD PUBLISHING COMPANY

CLEVELAND AND NEW YORK

God wove a web of loveliness,
Of clouds and stars and birds,
But made not anything at all
So beautiful as words.

—ANNA HEMPSTEAD BRANCH

AMERICAN WORDS

An Old Language in

a New World

When the first English settlers arrived in this country they were indeed in a New World. Everywhere they turned, they saw things that no one in the Old World had ever looked upon before. Trees of kinds they did not know came down to the water's edge. The dark-skinned natives who gazed silently at them as they came ashore from their ships were such people as no English men and women had ever before had as neighbors. Their bows and arrows, their clubs, their bits of clothing, their beads and other ornaments, their brush-and-bark hovels, were all new to these first English settlers. And, of course, the woods, fields, and streams around them teemed with wild creatures no European recognized.

It is certainly not remarkable that the language which the settlers brought with them began to change almost as soon as they reached shore on this side of the Atlantic. The colonists needed new words for a new way of life, and they were eager to do things in new ways in this land so far from where they had lived before. Besides, change was nothing new to the English language. The English have always been an active, enterprising people. They have been mentally alert, constantly engaged in learning and doing new things.

A living language reflects the mental and physical activities of those who use it. As people accomplish more and more in all walks of life, their language changes so as always to be abreast of their achievements. Nothing that has taken place in the English language in this country differs in kind from what it was thoroughly accustomed to during the thousand years of its existence before it was brought to America.

So many things have happened to the language in this country during the last 350 years that this book is necessarily only an introduction to the subject. The American words and phrases included here are only a sample of the enlargement the vocabulary has undergone in what is now the United States. This increase in the resources of the vocabulary has involved three things: new meanings for old words, new words, and new phrases.

OLD WORDS GET NEW MEANINGS

Any page of even a small dictionary shows that many words have more than one meaning. Though dictionaries do not usually point out the fact, many of the meanings they record originated on this side of the ocean.

One of the first words to which the settlers gave a new meaning was *Indian*. They brought the term from home where it had been used, originally, for a native of India, but later had come to be applied to a native of the present West Indies and Central America. This extension in the meaning of the word grew out of a mistake Columbus made in thinking he had reached India. Although he made four voyages to this country, Columbus died without knowing where he had been.

Believing they were natives of remote parts of India, Columbus called the strange people he found on this side of the ocean *Indios*. Accounts of his discoveries were quickly translated from Spanish into all the languages of Europe. His term became *Indians* in English and was used for those natives of the West Indies and Central America whom he had visited.

It was soon found that Columbus had been in error, but the mistake he made accounts for the fact that the first English-speaking settlers in what is now North Carolina and Virginia called the natives there by a name that had already been used for those hundreds of miles to the south. And *Indians* has spread so widely that it is now used for all the natives of North and South America, with the exception of the Eskimos in the far north and the Patagonians and the Fuegians in the extreme south.

Students and scholars have all along recognized that the use of the word *Indians* for native Americans is the result of a mistake and that a better term should be found. Sixty years ago a scholar coined *Amerind* to take its place. He made this word by taking parts of *American* and *Indian*. At the same time he suggested *Amerindian* to serve as an adjective in such expressions as "Amerindian tales and myths." These words are now often used by scholars, but the great majority of people never heard of them. *Indian* satisfies them perfectly.

It is pleasant to know that although Americans failed almost completely to give the natives of their own country a fitting name, they succeeded admirably with reference to the natives of the Philippine Islands. The first Spanish discoverers who visited those islands called the natives *Indios*, just as Columbus had done here a quarter of a century earlier. And the natives had this name until late in the nineteenth century when Americans in considerable numbers arrived in the Philippines. They did not call the people *Indians*, as they might well have done under the circumstances, but *Filipinos*, obviously the proper name for them.

Many old plant and animal names have been given new meanings in this country. Laurel as it is known in Europe is not native to America, but frontiersmen gave that name to various trees and shrubs that appeared to them to be laurel. The sycamore in this country is quite unlike the tree known in Europe by that name.

What we call a robin is really a thrush. The first settlers thought he looked like a bird which at home in England they knew as a robin, so they named him accordingly. Some of the early settlers in what is now Virginia and Maryland came upon a huge beast they thought was a buffalo, and they gave him that name. Scholars who came much later found that the creature is really a bison. But very few people call him by that name now, nor is it at all likely that anybody will ever refer to Buffalo Bill, the noted plainsman, as Bison Bill.

The first letter, A, of the English alphabet has been called on here to do additional duty by serving as a grade which pupils and students get in school when they make good records. Other letters from the first part of the alphabet are used in a similar way. So far as is now known, this use for the letters began at Augustana College in Rock Island, Illinois. The first teachers there were graduates of Swedish universities, and being accustomed to this use of the ABC's in Sweden, they introduced the custom at Augustana.

Grade has received new senses in American schools. Here pupils receive grades, but in England they get *marks*. American pupils are grouped into grades, and such expressions as *first grade, second grade, grade school, grade teacher*, are common. In this country teachers grade papers, but in England they "mark" them. *Class* is an old word that has had new uses given it here. Students are grouped into classes, and such expressions as *class day, class ring, class pin, class reunion*, are often used.

High School does not mean quite the same thing in the United States that it does in England. In some high schools, and regularly in college, American students form groups called *fraternities*. The first of these was formed at the College of William and Mary in Williamsburg, Virginia, about 1777. The students in the group thought of themselves as being brothers, and accordingly took an old word meaning "brotherhood" for the name of their club.

Later, women students felt the need of similar organizations, and at first called the groups they formed *fraternities* also. But the word in this sense did not suit very well. Too many people know that *fraternity* means "a brotherhood." So the girls gave it up, and followed the example of the boys by calling their organization a *sorority*, that is, "sisterhood," and so gave that old word a new meaning.

Elevator is an old word that has had new senses given it. It had been in the language more than a hundred years when an American mechanic, Oliver Evans, in 1787 invented an apparatus for lifting wheat or other grain from a lower to an upper floor in a mill by means of an endless belt to which very small buckets were attached. When he applied for a patent on his invention Evans called it an *elevator*. The same word was later used for a cage or car that takes people from one floor to another in a tall building. Still another use was found for the old word when it was used for a building made to store grain. Such a building is often called by its full name, *grain elevator*.

Perhaps there is nothing that contributes more to the health and happiness of a household than a refrigerator. Thomas Moore of Baltimore, Maryland, in 1803 invented a form of cooling chamber by making two large boxes, one inside the other. Between them he put insulating material, and then in the inner box he placed ice and such food as he wished to keep cold. He called this invention a *refrigerator*, thus giving a new meaning to an old word.

THOUSANDS OF NEW TERMS ARISE

The first settlers in this country and those who came after them could not take care of all their linguistic needs by giving new meanings to old words. They have had to find many entirely new terms. Especially they had to have names for villages, towns, cities, creeks, rivers, lakes, mountains, and plains, as well as suitable terms for the plants and animals they found all over the country. Americans have provided themselves with so many words of all kinds that no dictionary could possibly contain all of them. It is interesting to study the ways people through the years have gone about the task of securing new words.

One of the oldest and easiest ways to make a new word is to use two or more old words as one expression. Those who have spoken English through the centuries have employed this method so often that the language is abundantly supplied with such words as *alongside, anthill, backstairs, backstroke.* Often when two or more words are used together for a long time they lose their separate identities and merge into what appears to be a single word. One of the things that make dictionaries such interesting books is that they show that such words as *handicap, lord, ostrich, stirrup,* are made up of two or more words that have through long use melted together, as it were, into the forms they now have.

One of the first combinations made in this country was needed as a name for a small fur-bearing animal that quickly attracted the attention of the colonists at Jamestown. This brown, short-legged, ratlike creature was well known to the Indians, whose name for him sounded to the Jamestown settlers something like *mussascus, musquassus, muscassus,* as best they could express it. The result of their efforts to pronounce this hard Indian name was *musquash.*

This term did not appeal to all the settlers. Many of

them called the little creature a *muskrat,* a very good name
for him because he has the odor of musk about him and
looks somewhat like a large rat. Both these names, *musquash* and *muskrat,* have remained in use, but *muskrat*
is more familiar.

New combinations have been made by the hundreds in
providing names for American plants and animals. Often
the appearance of the new object or creature suggested a
good name for it. Such names as *bead snake, blacksnake,
copperhead, garter snake, green snake,* were obviously
suggested by the appearance of the snakes. Sometimes a
characteristic of the plant or animal suggested a name. The
rattlesnake was so named because of the hard, bony seg-
ments at the end of its tail which it rattles when alarmed.
The *milk snake* was thought by untrained observers to
drain cows of their milk. Not a single instance of this remarkable feat has ever been observed and is not likely to
be, but this name for a small, harmless snake often seen
about barnyards is still used.

Often the place where a thing was usually found suggested a name. Hundreds of names arose in this way, good
examples being *marsh hawk, marsh rabbit, marsh wren;
meadow beauty, meadow bird, meadow lark; mountain
goat, mountain laurel, mountain sheep; prairie dog, prairie
lily, prairie plover.*

Some words served extremely well as a base upon which
others were made by putting a term ahead of them. In this
way new expressions were easily made, such as *cat squirrel,
flying squirrel, fox squirrel; canvasback duck, ruddy duck,
wood duck.* The old word *berry* was used to form at least

a hundred such new terms, including *buffalo berry, china-berry, deerberry, fox berry, groundberry, hogberry, ink-berry, June berry, mooseberry, partridgeberry, pigeon berry, wolf berry.*

Terms of this kind were usually coined by people living out in the wilderness or countryside who had firsthand acquaintance with the things they named. But students and scholars were also busy making similar combinations involving the names of prominent people. Such terms as *Cooper's hawk, Audubon's warbler, Douglas fir, Bewick's wren, Bonaparte's gull, Lewis woodpecker, Wilson's snipe, Zenaida dove,* arose in this way.

Combinative terms were, of course, not limited to names for plants and animals. Such expressions as *clambake, close call, Columbus Day, common school, congressman, coonskin cap, cornhusking, cornstalk, cotton gin, double-header,* give a hint of the wide use of this method of securing new terms. *Coronary thrombosis, cosmic ray, cold war,* are good modern examples. So many people nowadays suffer from diseases involving the heart that *coronary thrombosis* is already widely known, though it did not come into the language until 1912, being first used by Dr. James B. Herrick, of Chicago, one of the foremost heart specialists of his day. Professor Robert A. Millikan of the California Institute of Technology first used *cosmic ray* in 1925. *Cold war* was coined in 1946 by H. B. Swope, a New York publicist and journalist.

The English language is well supplied with suffixes, and Americans have used many of them in making new terms. *Addressee, draftee, goatee; Americanism, colonist, isola-*

tionist; gangster, teamster; piker, zipper, were first used in this country and show clearly how they were made up.

Some suffixes have been used in making names for inhabitants of the various states. Two suffixes, *-an* and *-ian,* have led all the others in popularity. *Californian, Georgian, Mississippian, Missourian, New Mexican, Virginian; Arkansan, Coloradan, Idahoan, Ohioan, Utahan,* are examples of the use of these suffixes.

Other suffixes have been used with the names of some of the states. *Marylander, New Yorker, Rhode Islander, Vermonter; Wisconsinite, Wyomingite,* are examples. In some states usage is divided. A citizen of New Jersey may be known as a *Jerseyman* or a *Jerseyite,* just as one from New Hampshire may be a *New Hampshireman* or *New Hampshirite.*

Words are so personal that it is not surprising that in some states people take sides for or against certain terms of this kind. *Indianian* has been used for over a century for a person living in Indiana, but in 1922 a historian of the state expressed dissatisfaction with it and hoped *Indianan* might be used in its place. His main objection to *Indianian* was that in many words the putting of *-i-* where it is not needed is a sign of ignorance. He listed such forms as mountain*ious,* stupend*ious,* portent*ious,* as showing the undesirable tendency in pronunciation "to jab an *i* into the vitals of a word where it does not belong." Apparently most people now agree that *Indianan* is preferable.

The term *Michigander* is an oddity. It appears to have a suffix *-der,* but there is no such suffix, nor was this term

made by adding -der to Michigan. Michigander came
about in an unusual manner.

General Lewis Cass of Michigan was a candidate in the
presidential election of 1848. In the enthusiasm and excitement which usually accompanies such elections there was
much silly joke-making about the name of General Cass.
One of the foolish things said about his name was that it
really means "goose." Some now-unknown rhymester wrote
a political song the chorus of which was:

> Oh, then look here; oh, then look where?
> In Michigan right yander;
> Do not you see old Lewis Cass,
> He looks just like a gander!

This association of General Cass with a gander was considered a fine joke by his political opponents, and it was
not long before he was being referred to as a Michigander,
a nickname obviously made from Michigan and gander.
The term proved so popular that it has survived as a name
for any citizen of Michigan.

Some people feel that Michigander should be avoided as
uncomplimentary, and they prefer to use Michiganite.
H. L. Mencken, a diligent student of American terms, objected to Michigander because "it inspires idiots to call a
Michigan woman a Michigoose and a child a Michigos-
ling." But there is no evidence that those who live in
Michigan are as sensitive on this point as Mr. Mencken
thought they might be.

In making new words Americans have often taken other
words, or pieces of them, and from the fragments made a

term that served their purpose. *Amerind* and *Amerindian* were arrived at in this manner. *Motel* was made from *motorist* and *hotel,* and *motorcade* from *motorcar* and *cavalcade.* The scientist who coined *Technicolor* had studied at the Massachusetts Institute of Technology and used a little of the name of the school in the word he made.

One of the most interesting of the words Americans have made from pieces of others is seen in *Hubam clover,* a term now in the larger dictionaries and well known to farmers in some parts of the country. In 1913 two plants of an annual type of white sweet clover were found in one of the test plots at the Iowa Experiment Station at Ames, Iowa. These plants greatly surprised those who found them, for up to that time nothing was known of an annual type of white sweet clover.

Professor Harold D. Hughes at Ames investigated this clover so successfully that in 1919 he found it had developed on an old plantation not far from Uniontown, Alabama. A scientist who knew of the work Professor Hughes had done suggested that this new clover be called *Hubam clover,* a name that alludes to Professor *Hu*ghes and to Ala*bam*a.

In coining new terms Americans have sometimes taken parts of old words and made new ones of them. *Telegram* was coined in 1852 from *tele-* and *-gram.* When it first appeared, it provoked a famous Cambridge University scholar who denounced it as a barbarism, and much preferred *telegrapheme* which he said was "a rightly constructed word." Few people felt this scholar's aversion to *telegram,* but he always spoke of sending a *telegrapheme,* never a *telegram.*

Sometimes it is easier to borrow a word from another language than it is to make up a new one. Americans have taken many words from the languages of those with whom they have associated in this country.

Perhaps the earliest term taken from the Indians who lived in what is now the United States is *Roanoke.* It was borrowed in July, 1584, by explorers sent out by Sir Walter Raleigh. Queen Elizabeth had given him the right to settle lands in the New World, and he at once organized an exploring party which reached an island off the coast of what is now North Carolina.

The newcomers asked the natives the name of the island, but the Indians had no idea at all of what the strange pale-faced men wanted. The best the islanders could do was to utter their own name, hoping that would satisfy the inquirers. The explorers went their way, thinking they had the information desired, and wrote down the name of the island as *Roanoac, Ronoke, Ronoak.* It is still called *Roanoke Island.* The same Indian word, used by the natives as a tribal name with some such meaning as "northern people," has been useful in naming towns and counties and rivers as well as Roanoke Sound off the coast of North Carolina.

Indian terms are abundant in American English, especially proper names such as *Allegheny, Apache, Appalachian, Appomattox, Cherokee, Chesapeake, Chicago, Chickasaw, Erie, Iroquois, Manhattan, Monongahela,*

Natchez, Niagara, Omaha, Potomac, Poughkeepsie, Rappahannock, Sioux, Wabash. Of the fifty states now in the Union twenty-seven have Indian names. But not all the words from Indian sources are proper names. There are many common terms, such as *hickory, hominy, moccasin, moose, papoose, pecan, persimmon, squash, squaw, tepee, terrapin, tomahawk, wampum, wigwam.*

It should be borne in mind that the Indians north of Mexico spoke no less than forty or more languages when Europeans first arrived here. Many of the sounds in these languages were entirely unlike those any of the newcomers had ever heard. When a European listened to an Indian speak, he naturally related the sound the native made to those in his own language. In doing so, he often misunderstood or misinterpreted what the Indian said. When a European reduced an Indian word to writing, he did as well as he could by using the letters of his alphabet.

The result is that terms of Indian origin in present-day English are seldom preserved in forms that could be recognized by any Indian who ever lived. The melodious quality heard in many Indian words has in large measure been given to them in the process of making them English.

The significance or meaning of Indian words is often difficult or impossible to find out. The natives did not have any written literature, and they were quite ignorant of the basic meanings of many words they used. Indian languages also borrowed from each other, and this, too, increased the difficulties of students who study their languages.

Whenever in this book or elsewhere a meaning is ventured for an Indian term, the probability is that it is a guess and not to be taken too seriously. *Chicago* seems to have a meaning more clearly established than usual. A French explorer who visited the region in 1688 said the natives called it *Chicagou* because of the abundance of wild onions growing there. Students have thought it was the disagreeable odor of the pink blossoms of the little wild onions that inspired the Indian name, and that "place of the bad smell" or "place of the skunk" might be more accurate interpretations of the name. On the other hand, those anxious to defend the name of the city insist that its name as the Indians thought of it signified merely "strong," and that "Strong-town" is much nearer the proper sense. Thus do research and jest and imagination play upon many Indian terms, and it soon becomes impossible to sift out of the result the grain of truth, if any, from which it all began.

But the Indian languages were by no means the only source of borrowings at the disposal of those who spoke English in this country. People from the far corners of the world have had a part in making the United States. To give a detailed indication of the borrowings made from all the languages represented here would require a very large book indeed.

A brief listing of some of the borrowings will suggest what the complete story would be like. From the Dutch have come such words as *cooky, Santa Claus, sleigh, stoop, waffle.* The Germans have contributed such words as *delicatessen, frankfurter, nix, pretzel, sauerkraut, semester, zwieback.* Such words as *caribou, chowder, cigarette, picayune, prairie, rayon, restaurant,* clearly show the influence of the French. Of all the European languages from which American English has borrowed, Spanish leads all the rest. Such words as *avocado, bonanza, bronco, pueblo, sombrero, stampede, vamoose,* and a great many more are from this source.

Words like *banjo, gumbo, pickaninny, voodoo,* show that people from Africa have made their contribution to the English used in the United States. *Chop suey, chow mein,* indicate that there have been Chinese working here with us. *Malamute, mukluk, parka,* come to us from the Eskimo, just as *hula, Kanaka, ukulele,* come from Hawaii, and *kudzu, nisei, tycoon,* from Japan.

Ancient languages as well as modern ones have been drawn upon by Americans to make new words. *Alumnus,* a young man who has graduated from college, is an old term, but *alumna,* the feminine form of the word, came into use in this country only about seventy-five years ago. *Immigrant* and *immigration* are much older, but they too came from Latin, as did *tractor,* and *vireo.*

One of the most common of the words borrowed from Greek came into the language in 1910. Dr. Henry H. Goddard, a member of the American Association for the Study of the Feeble-Minded, was a member of a committee attempting to classify people of less than normal intelligence. In the course of his work he felt the need for a term for those unfortunates whose mental age is from eight to twelve years. He wrote:

> Therefore it became necessary to discover a new term. *Idiot* and *imbecile* are both Greek. A Greek word would make it uniform. But I could think of none. I appealed to my friends and got many suggestions, all the way from

deviates to *the almosts!* One day there dropped into my mind *oxymoron*, with its interesting etymology, "sharp-foolish"; then I thought of *sophomore*—the "wise fool." Turning to my Greek lexicon, I found *moros—mora—moron*, "dull, stupid, silly, foolish," a perfect description of our 8-12 year-group.

NEW PHRASES ORIGINATE

In expanding the resources of the English language, Americans have introduced hundreds of phrases, many of which have become obsolete, though a great many have remained.

Phrases are, of course, nothing new to the English language. Dictionaries include a great many of them, and when possible explain the circumstances under which they were first used. As a rule they are of a colloquial or slang nature, and quite often cannot be explained logically. When the real explanation of a phrase is not at hand, people indulge in stories of how they think it might have come about.

American pioneers invented many expressions having to do with animals. A child too eager or impatient about something might be told, "just *hold your horses* a minute." This encouragement to patience might be changed to *hold your potato.*

In frontier times every farmer was his own butcher. Often he selected a fine cold spell during the winter and invited neighbors to come in and assist with the butchering. And they came with pleasure—men, women, and children. As they engaged in butchering the fat hogs of their neighbor, they had a good time together with plenty to eat, including the most delicious portions of the freshly slaughtered hogs. These occasions were so pleasant that *to have a hog-killing time of it* used to be readily understood as meaning to have a very good time indeed.

Part of the work of butchering involved salting the meat before putting it away for future use. The expression *to salt down* came into use for laying anything away in a safe place with the idea of making use of it later. If a child became too fresh or saucy, his parents might *salt him down* by administering a severe scolding or a sound spanking.

When a young man anxious to make a good impression on his sweetheart treated her mother with marked kindness, he was said to be *salting the cow to catch the calf.* Often boys or girls showing little promise of ever becoming useful or substantial citizens turn out to be exceptionally fine men and women. Pioneers called attention to this possibility by saying, "*Nobody knows the luck of a lousy calf.*"

In a country which abounded with wild animals it was natural for many expressions referring to them to come into use. At one time the beaver was one of the most widely distributed animals in this country and the one most eagerly sought for its fur. *To work like a beaver, or to be as busy* (or *industrious*) *as a beaver* were expressions that alluded to the industry of this forest creature. Although the beaver is rated as having only half as much intelligence as a horse, it is not easily trapped. If a frontiersman wished to praise a man's intelligence and cleverness, he might say he was *up to beaver,* that is, he was "smart enough to catch a beaver." One lacking in experience or caution was *not up to beaver.*

Bears disappeared from England hundreds of years before the first settlers reached this country, where these animals were quite common. The bad humor of a bear was alluded to in such expressions as *as cross as a bear, as mad as a beaten bear. Bring on your bears* was a frontier challenge of defiance, an invitation to an adversary to do his worst. Hornets resembled bears in being often out of humor, so the expression *as mad as a hornet* was frequently used.

In early times turkeys were so abundant that many expressions arose about them. Some of these are now difficult to account for or even to understand. Anyone *as poor as Job's turkey* was very poor indeed. Why Job and a turkey were associated cannot now be made out, for that patient man certainly never owned a turkey. *To talk turkey* is to speak with the utmost plainness. How this term came into use is unknown.

An effort to account for it was made more than a hundred years ago. A white man and an Indian went hunting, so it was said, and killed nothing but a crow and a turkey. In dividing the spoils the white man generously told the Indian, "You may take your choice. You take the crow and I'll take the turkey. Or, if you'd rather, I'll take the turkey and you take the crow." The Indian reflected a moment on his friend's generosity, and replied, "Ugh! You no talk turkey to me a bit!"

Not to say peaturkey to anybody was to keep silent.

What a "peaturkey" is has not so far been found out. *To say turkey to one and buzzard to another* was to give one an advantage over another. *To be as proud as a lame turkey* is an expression of puzzling meaning. Possibly it was an ironic way of referring to one exceedingly depressed or humbled.

Owls inspired a good many expressions, most of them now obsolete. *As solemn as an owl in black, to stare like an owl in a thunder shower, to be a caution to hoarse owls, to feel like a stewed owl, to be as drunk as a boiled owl,* are a few of the terms this creature inspired.

Snakes were so common and so universally dreaded by most people that many expressions involving them grew up among settlers on the frontier. *To work like killing snakes* was to work very hard. *To see snakes* or *to have snakes in one's boots* was to suffer from indulgence in strong drink. *Wake snakes and walk your chalks* was an expression of jubilation.

Bark played an important role in the lives of the first settlers. It was used so much that it is found in many expressions, such as *bark cabin, bark camp, bark canoe, bark hut, bark shanty, bark wigwam.* Many colloquial phrases involving bark came into use, some of which are still current. *To take the bark off* a person is to give him a sound thrashing or tongue-lashing. *To talk with the bark on* is to speak with the utmost plainness and emphasis. *To talk the bark off a tree* is to talk much and enthusiastically. *To be tighter than the bark on a tree* is to be extremely stingy.

Beans were widely grown and used on the frontier.

They were so abundant as to be worth very little. To say a thing was *not worth a hill of beans* or did *not amount to a hill of beans* was a way of emphasizing its worthlessness. *Not to know beans* was to be entirely ignorant. *Not to say beans* about a matter was not to mention it at all.

This has been only a brief glimpse into some of the methods used in the United States, to modify and enlarge the vocabulary of the English language to make it better serve the needs of the American people. Just as those living in Canada, Australia, Africa, and India have made some changes in the English they use, so people in the United States of America have, in the main unconsciously, differed in their ways of expressing themselves from those living elsewhere. An excellent way to learn about an individual or about people in general is to pay close attention to their language.

American Words

✧

AIR BRAKE   Almost as soon as trains came into use, the problem of how to stop them became a difficult one. Everyone, it seemed, had ideas on the subject, for there were hundreds of patents taken out for various kinds of brakes before 1869, when George Westinghouse secured his first patent on a remarkable brake operated by compressed air.

At first he had great difficulty in getting anyone, even his own father, interested in what he was trying to do. Railroad men were hard to convince that air could stop a train. They relied on *brakemen,* as they are called, who applied each brake by hand. When he was still a long way from a station, the engineer would whistle "down brakes" to signal the brakemen to get busy. They rushed from car to car, turning heavy horizontal handwheels which slowly tightened chains that in turn pulled brake shoes against pairs of wheels. The brakemen on freight trains had to run along on top of the cars in all kinds of weather, freezing in winter, and sometimes missing their footing and falling between the cars on windy, slippery nights. The brakes on some cars would be set tighter than on others,

31

causing the cars to bump violently against each other with much discomfort and some danger to passengers.

Air brakes, on the other hand, operate so smoothly and quickly that even on a freight train a mile long all of them can be applied by the engineer in a few seconds. The name *atmospheric brake* was at first given this remarkable invention, but the shorter term now in use soon took its place.

AMERICAN   It is embarrassing that the citizens of the United States do not have a satisfactory name. In the Declaration of Independence, the British colonists called their country the *United States of America*. In adopting this excellent name, they created a difficulty. What should an inhabitant of a country with such a long name be called?

For more than 150 years those living in this country have searched in vain for a suitable name for themselves. In 1803, a prominent American physician, Dr. Samuel L. Mitchill, suggested that the entire country be called *Fredonia*, or *Fredon*. He had taken the English term *freedom* and the Latin *colonia*, meaning "a colony or settlement," and from them coined *Fredonia*, of which *Fredon* is a short form.

Dr. Mitchill thought that with this word as the name for the country as a whole, the derivative *Fredish* would follow naturally, corresponding to *British*, *Turkish*, *Spanish*, and the like. In the same way, he thought *Frede* would be a good name for an inhabitant of Fredonia. But his fellow citizens laughed at the doctor's names and never used any of them.

Much earlier *Columbia,* in allusion to Columbus the discoverer, had been used of our country, and many people were in favor of it. The District of Columbia received its name when the name *Columbia* was at the height of its popularity. But in 1819 one of the countries of South America was named *Colombia,* so the chances of *Columbia* being used here went to pieces at once.

Such citizen names as *United Statesian,* shortened to *Unisian,* and *United Statian* were proposed but quickly abandoned and forgotten. No better success has greeted *Usona* (from United States of North America) as a name for the country, and *Usonian* as a term for a citizen of it.

Usage overwhelmingly favors *American* as a name for an inhabitant of the United States of America, though all Americans realize it covers far too much territory.

ANESTHESIA   Sometimes a word has an excellent opportunity to come into use, but fails to take advantage of it. Then later, under different circumstances, the same word is introduced again and becomes popular at once.

Anesthesia, then spelled *anaesthesia* appeared in an English dictionary as early as 1721. It was defined as "a Defect of Sensation, as in Paralytic and blasted [that is, stricken] Persons." There is no indication that anybody paid the slightest attention to this learned term. In 1755 when Samuel Johnson brought out his large dictionary of the English language he did not even include it.

But on October 16, 1846, a remarkable thing took place in Boston. A young dentist, William T. G. Morton, had become locally famous for extracting teeth painlessly. He rendered his patients temporarily unconscious by having them breathe the vapor of a liquid, the nature of which he did not care to reveal. He was invited to come to the Massachusetts General Hospital and help in an operation on a young man who had to have a tumor removed from his neck.

Dr. Morton accepted the invitation, and the operation was entirely painless. The young man quickly recovered and felt no bad effects from his most unusual experience. Other operations followed with equally satisfactory results. Doctors all over Boston were greatly excited about what had taken place. They realized that a new age in surgery was at hand.

Among those who were impressed by the new discovery was Dr. Oliver Wendell Holmes. On November 21, 1846, he wrote a letter to Morton giving him "a hint or two as to the names, or the name, to be applied to the state produced, and to the agent." He suggested that the state of unconsciousness on the part of the patient should be called *anesthesia*.

For the second time this word, originally a Greek one, had its chance to become English. And this time it caught on at once. It went all over the world along with the news of the remarkable discovery made in Boston. And to

Holmes, rather than to the dictionary of 1721, we are in-
debted for this convenient term.

For the story of a much less successful word growing
out of Dr. Morton's work see p. 133.

ANNIE OAKLEY   If pretty Anne Mozee had
not had an unusual husband, her professional name would
never have become a part of the English language. When
quite young she married Frank E. Butler, an expert marks-
man who was traveling with a show and giving exhibitions
of his skill in shooting.

Naturally Mr. Butler encouraged his girl-wife to become interested in what he did, and he was delighted to
find she had a talent for shooting. She was soon able to
take the place of his assistant on the stage. In only a short
time she was a better shot than her husband!

He gallantly recognized her superiority, and knew that
she was more attractive on the stage than he. So he grace-
fully relinquished to her the leading role in their act and
became her manager. He realized that she needed a good
stage name. It is said that in looking through a Chicago
street directory he came upon *Oakley Boulevard,* and
at once fancied *Oakley.* She made her new name, *Annie
Oakley,* famous both in this country and in Europe.

She and her husband traveled for many years with
Buffalo Bill's Wild West Show, and she gave performances
before many of the notables of Europe, including Queen
Victoria of England. The Crown Prince of Germany re-
quested her to shoot a cigarette from his lips, and she

obliged, much to the consternation of the royal household. Before her death in 1926 at the age of sixty-six, she had the pleasure of knowing that *Annie Oakley* had become part of the English language in the sense of a free pass to any kind of show or entertainment. It is thought this use of her show name grew out of the punctured condition in which she left her targets. They looked like admission tickets generously perforated by the ticket taker's punch.

APPALOOSA HORSE   When French explorers first came among the Indians in the northeastern part of what is now the State of Oregon, they found these natives had remarkably beautiful spotted horses.

The Indians were the Nez Percés (that is, "pierced-nose ones,") and many of them lived in a region of extensive grassy plains. The French word for a grassy plain is *pelouse,* so Canadian-French *voyageurs* referred to such horses as these Indians raised as being "à palousé," that is, from the grassy plains. Taking the hint from the French, those who spoke English called such horses *Appaloosas.*

This horse is liberally sprinkled with black-and-white spots, some of them mere specks but others three or four inches in diameter. Usually the spots are mainly about the hips. They have much white in their eyes, just as human beings do. And their hoofs are marked with vertical black-and-white stripes.

So many of these horses were killed in frontier wars that it looked as if they might all disappear. But in 1928 some lovers of horses organized the Appaloosa Horse Club at

Moscow, Idaho, and have taken special care of these famous horses. Now once more there are thousands of them. They are becoming more and more widely known, especially through the use of them in motion pictures.

APPENDICITIS   If you felt ill someday with pain in the abdomen and a horrible nausea, and the doctor said you were suffering from an attack of *typhlitis, perityphlitis,* or *peritonitis appendicularis localis,* you would no doubt be greatly alarmed.

The reason no doctor will ever disturb you in this way is that in 1886 Dr. Reginald Heber Fitz, a professor at the Harvard Medical School, published a sensational article in the *American Journal of Medical Science.*

Dr. Fitz had made a careful study of the disease that was known by one or the other of the learned names just mentioned. He dissected no less than five hundred persons who had died in various stages of this terrible ailment, and in nearly every case he had found that the inflammation characteristic of it had started in the appendix. He was convinced from what he had found that *typhlitis* and the other names up to that time in use gave the wrong impression of the nature of the disease. He suggested that *appendicitis,* that is, "inflammation of the appendix," would be a much more preferable term.

This remarkable article by Dr. Fitz is now regarded as a medical classic. It revolutionized the treatment of the disease with which it dealt, and it ushered a new word, *appendicitis,* into the English language.

Some of Dr. Fitz's friends joked him for having made a new word a little unscientifically. *Appendix* is of Latin origin, but the *-itis* which Fitz added to it is a Greek termination denoting a disease or inflammation. When a word is ideally made, the parts of it are from the same language. But the number of words that are hybrids made of elements coming from different languages is quite large, and *appendicitis* has not suffered at all in its usefulness from its mixed parentage.

ARBOR DAY   Early settlers in this country had to cut down millions of fine trees in clearing fields and making homes. In later times their descendants began to make up for this earlier wastefulness by planting trees.

In 1872, J. Sterling Morton and others who thought as he did, succeeded in getting the Board of Agriculture in Nebraska to set aside the tenth day of April for tree planting, and to name this day *Arbor Day*. *Arbor* is a Latin word meaning "tree," so this expression means "Tree Day." Those who use *Arbor Day* are speaking a little Latin, though they may not realize it.

On the first Arbor Day in Nebraska, April 10, 1872, more than a million trees were set out. Now such a day is observed throughout the United States and in Puerto Rico.

AX, *to have an ax to grind*   On September 7, 1810, the following story appeared in a Pennsylvania newspaper.

When I was a little boy, Messrs. Printers, I remember one cold winter's morning, I was accosted by a smiling man, with an ax on his shoulder.

"My pretty boy," said he, "has your father a grindstone?"

"Yes, sir," said I.

"You are a fine little fellow," said he, "will you let me grind my ax on it?" Pleased with his compliment of "fine little fellow"—

"O, yes, sir," I answered, "it is down in the shop."

"And will you, my man," said he, patting me on the head, "get a little hot water?" How could I refuse? I ran and soon brought a kettle full.

"How old are you, and what's your name," continued he without waiting for a reply. "I am sure you are one of the finest lads that I have ever seen, will you just turn a few minutes for me?"

Tickled with the flattery like a little fool I went to work, and bitterly did I rue the day. It was a new ax, and I toiled and tugged, till I was almost tired to death. The school bell rang, and I could not get away,—my hands were blistered, and it was not half ground. At length, however, the ax was sharpened, and the man turned to me with—

"Now, you little rascal, you've played the truant,—scud to school, or you'll rue it."

Alas, thought I, it was hard enough to turn grindstone this cold day, but to be called "little rascal" was too much. It sank deep in my mind, and often have I thought of it since.

This little story found its way into school readers of the time, and became widely known. It was not long until the expression *to have an ax to grind* was widely understood as denoting that someone had a selfish purpose to serve, and was using flattery to secure what he wished.

BAKING POWDER   Settlers in this country soon found that wheat grows remarkably well here, but they failed to make good bɪ ˙ᵈ from it, because they had no leavening agent. At home they had been accustomed to yeast in some form, but in the American wilderness there was no yeast. Bread made without something to make it rise is heavy and soggy.

Housewives in New England soon found that the dregs or sediments of wine, beer, or cider could be used to make bread lighter. They called this yeasty sediment *emptins*, or *emptin yeast*, apparently because in England they had been familiar with the expression *brewers' emptyings*, meaning "a form of yeast made at breweries." Some of the women found that a good form of emptins could be made from milk which had been allowed to sour. They called this product *milk emptins*.

They made emptins out of a number of things, especially from the juice of boiled hops. Hops grow on an attractive climbing vine that makes an excellent shade. Settlers saw to it that they had plenty of hop vines growing around their homes. Germans in Pennsylvania called liquid yeast made from hops *sots*, this name being derived from the German word *Satz*, meaning "sediments or dregs."

Another discovery was that well-salted flour or cornmeal batter or dough mixed with water or milk has yeasty properties and can be used in bread-making. Housewives called this crude form of yeast *salt-rising,* and they spoke of *salt-rising bread,* a form of bread which under this name still appeals to the taste of many people.

Over a century ago some clever chemist in this country found that he could take a form of potassium and make from it a preparation which would at once begin to release the air imprisoned in it when anything slightly acid, such as milk, was poured over it. This preparation, it was found, could be improved by making it with sodium. As early as 1837 it was sold in stores as *saleratus.* The first part of this name is the Latin word for salt, seen in such common words as *sal*ad and *sal*ary. The meaning of *saleratus* is, literally, "salt with air imprisoned in it."

Constant efforts to improve this product led to the preparation of what was called at first *yeast powder.* This expression had been used earlier in England for yeast in a dried and powdered form, but here it was used for what soon became much better known as *baking powder.*

Emptins, emptin yeast, milk emptins, saleratus, salt-rising, sots, yeast powder, are traces left in the language by the efforts of Americans to have good bread. So essential is baking powder and its skillful use to a happy household that someone has said with reference to the success of girls in getting good husbands: "It takes face powder to catch them, but baking powder to hold them."

BALD EAGLE   This eagle received his name because when he is fully grown the feathers on his head and neck are snow-white and give him, when seen at a distance, the appearance of being bald. Like so many other birds of importance, however, he has received a number of other names, such as *bird of freedom, bird of Washington, brown eagle, calumet eagle, gray eagle, national bird, nun's eagle, white-headed eagle,* and *American eagle.*

A committee appointed by the Second Continental Congress to suggest a design for the great seal of our country decided to use a representation of this fine bird on it. Public opinion was not unanimous that this eagle should be honored in this way, because he is a robber.

He often sits on a lofty perch and watches a fish hawk busily at work trying to secure a meal. When the smaller bird has caught a choice fish and is carrying it home, this big fellow swoops down and so frightens the poor fish hawk that it drops its prey and makes off as fast as possible. The eagle then catches the falling fish in midair and has it for his own.

But the majestic looks of the bird, his seven-foot wingspread, and his ability to take care of himself carried the day in his favor. His picture appears not only on the great seal of the United States, but also on many of the bills and coins used in this country. He is the most pictured bird in the world.

Among the finest things ever written about the bald eagle are the following lines by John Burroughs, the American naturalist:

> He draws great lines across the sky; he sees the forests like a carpet beneath him; he sees the hills and valleys as folds and wrinkles in a many-colored tapestry; he sees the

river as a silver belt connecting remote horizons. We climb mountain-peaks to get a glimpse of the spectacle that is hourly spread out beneath him. Dignity, elevation, repose, are his. I would have my thoughts take as wide a sweep. I would be as far removed from petty cares and turmoils of this noisy and blustering world.

BALL, *to be behind the eight ball*   The best explanation of this slang expression is that it arose from a form of pool called *Kelly pool.* In this game the player has to knock fifteen numbered balls into the pockets at the corners of the pool table. The rules of the game as it is sometimes played make it necessary to pocket the balls in the order of their numbers with the exception of ball number eight, which must be the last one pocketed.

Sometimes the eight ball gets in between the cue ball, which the player uses in striking the others, and the ball which has to be pocketed next. When this happens, the player is in a difficult spot. He is not permitted to touch the eight ball, and yet he has to hit the ball behind it. Under such circumstances he tries a "cushion shot," that is, he drives his cue ball against the cushioned side of the table, hoping it will bounce away at such an angle as to strike the ball he is interested in and leave the eight ball undisturbed.

From this situation, so it is said, the expression *to be behind the eight ball* arose.

BATHYSPHERE   Students of words would certainly appreciate it if those who coin new terms would be so thoughtful as to tell just how they went about the matter. Fortunately such an explanation is available for *bathysphere*, a word so new that it has not yet made its way into all the dictionaries.

It was coined in 1930 by Dr. William Beebe, a scientist and author who became greatly interested in studying the animal life at the bottom of the sea. He soon became eager to go down into the sea as far as he possibly could and observe the animals that lived there.

With the aid of a friend, he designed a large, hollow steel sphere, 54 inches in diameter on the inside, the shell being about one and a half inches thick. Fully equipped with a four-hundred-pound door, and with two quartz windows three inches thick and eight inches in diameter, this apparatus weighed about five thousand pounds. It was certainly large enough to have a name. Dr. Beebe wrote:

> As the great chamber took shape, we found the need of a definite name. We spoke of it casually and quite incorrectly as tank and cylinder and bell. One day, when I was writing the name of a deep-sea fish—*Bathytroctes*—the appropriateness of the Greek prefix occurred to me; I coined the word *Bathysphere*, and the name has stuck.

Dr. Beebe's word is well-made according to the most exacting standards. Both parts of it—*bathy-*, meaning "deep," and -*sphere*—are from the Greek. The name of the fish that suggested that of the apparatus is also well-made and means "deep (or deep-sea) nibbler."

BAY LYNX   The first settlers at Jamestown in 1607 found that in the forest about them lived a catlike animal which the Indians told them was a "vetchun-quoyes." This name was very hard for the colonists to pronounce, so they called the creature a *wildcat*, in this way using a name well-known to them, but mistakenly giving it to an animal different from the European one of the same name.

In Canada, French fur traders found a larger cousin of the Jamestown creature and called it a *loup-cervier*, that is, "deer wolf," this being the French for a lynx.

Colonists in New England, becoming acquainted with both these animals, borrowed the French name; but they could not pronounce *loup-cervier* very well. The spellings they used show the difficulty they had: *louservia, leusifee, lucive, lucervee,* and even *Lucy-V!* Finally in their struggles they arrived at *lucifer,* a name they could pronounce. So one of the local names for the northern cat and its closely related southern cousin is *lucifer.*

Both these animals have very short tails, and after a time it occurred to someone to call the southern creature a *bob-tailed cat.* This was soon cut down to *bobcat,* a name that is now becoming increasingly common.

But perhaps the best name for both these creatures is *bay lynx,* for they are lynxes and of a reddish-brown, or bay, color. The northern one, however, is usually called a *Canada lynx,* or *Canadian lynx.* But such names as *mountain cat, red lynx,* and *spotted tiger* are also used for these closely related animals.

BEE   In pioneer times, settlers often came together to give a neighbor a day's help with building his
house, clearing a field, husking corn, getting the stones
out of a field, and other chores. Women would assemble
to spin all day or make a quilt or put up apple butter for
one of their number.

The name they gave these gatherings for neighborly
help was *bee,* so they had *apple bees, husking bees,
logging bees, quilting bees, raising bees, stone bees,* and
many others.

Bee as used here is puzzling. It is probably not the word
for the well-known insect. The custom to which it refers
did not originate here, for the country people of England
were accustomed to giving free help to each other in
harvesting, haymaking, and the like. They called this
voluntary help *boon,* a term well-known in the sense of
a favor or reward.

This *boon* was pronounced in various ways in different
parts of the English countryside. The spellings of it do not
give just the information needed, but forms like *beun,
bean, been,* are sufficient to cause one to suspect that *bee,*
the form popular in this country, is a variant of *boon.*

BELITTLE   Many of the words which were
first used in this country were ridiculed when they first
appeared in print. About 1780 Thomas Jefferson coined
belittle, and the critics at once condemned it as a perfectly ridiculous term.

Noah Webster did not share in the hostility toward *belittle*. He included it in his dictionary of 1828 without comment of any kind. About twenty years after his death, however, in a new edition of his dictionary a note was added to the word: [*Rare* in America. *Not used* in England.]

In 1872 a distinguished American scholar decided the time had come to kill *belittle*, which he came upon often in his reading. So he roundly and soundly denounced the term and concluded with these words: "It has no visible chance of becoming English; and as the more critical writers of America, like all those of Great Britain, feel no need of it, the sooner it is abandoned to the incurably vulgar, the better."

The professor was entirely unsuccessful in his efforts to destroy *belittle*. It is now a standard word wherever English is used. And it has given rise to two other terms often used: *belittler* and *belittling*.

BLACK WIDOW   Those acquainted with this unlovely poisonous creature have used many names for it. Here are some of them:

black spider	pokomoo
black widow	red-spotted spider
deadly spider	shoe-button spider
hourglass spider	southern spider
long-legged spider	T-dot spider
poison lady	T-spider

Four of these names may be regarded as the best of those so far suggested.

Black widow at the present time seems to be leading in the race for popularity. It was given the spider because the females have the reputation of killing and eating their husbands. No doubt they have earned this reputation, but it is also true that sometimes the husband pounces on his wife and eats her!

Hourglass spider is a good name too, because a dark-red marking on the underside of the female spider is shaped something like an hourglass.

Pokomoo is not widely used, being restricted to parts of California. It is an Indian name and what it signifies is not known. The Indians who used it thought the spider scratched people sometimes with one of its long legs and that the scratch made a bad sore. Some of the California Indians used the poison of this spider on the tips of their arrows.

Shoe-button spider is another good name. For older people it is a pleasant reminder of the time when button shoes were quite popular. The round, glossy body of this spider is about the size and color of buttons formerly used on shoes.

BOBOLINK   It is all right for a person to have two names, one his real name and the other his pen name or perhaps his business or professional name. But if he has half a dozen, which he uses as it suits his convenience, the police are perhaps looking for him.

The bobolink has more than a dozen names, and yet he runs no risk of being arrested as a suspicious character. Some of his names come from his note, the most dignified one of these being *Robert of Lincoln*. This name is the title of a poem about the bird, written by William Cullen Bryant. The first two stanzas of this poem are:

> Merrily swinging on brier and weed,
>   Near to the nest of his little dame,
> Over the mountain-side or mead,
>   Robert of Lincoln is telling his name:
>   Bob-o'-link, bob-o'-link,
>   Spink, spank, spink;
> Snug and safe is that nest of ours,
> Hidden among the summer flowers,
>   Chee, chee, chee.
>
> Robert of Lincoln is gayly drest,
>   Wearing a bright black wedding-coat;
> White are his shoulders and white his crest,
>   Hear him call in his merry note:
>   Bob-o'-link, bob-o'-link,
>   Spink, spank, spink;
> Look, what a nice new coat is mine,
> Sure there was never a bird so fine,
>   Chee, chee, chee.

Here are some other names the bobolink has: *American ortolan, Maybird, meadow bird, reedbird, ricebird, skunk bird, white-winged blackbird.*

BOLL WEEVIL   The name which this insect now has is much shorter than the one originally given him.

At first he was the *Mexican cotton-boll weevil*. He received the first part of this name because he came into this country from Mexico, crossing the Rio Grande River near Brownsville, Texas, about 1892. The fact that he destroys young cotton bolls and looks somewhat like a weevil accounts for the rest of his name.

Although he is only about one fourth of an inch long and perhaps a third as wide, he has caused Southern cotton growers to lose millions of dollars. Oddly enough, the severe damage he did caused the farmers in one community in the South to build a monument of appreciation to him. When the weevil first appeared in that community, the farmers thought they were utterly ruined, for cotton had been for many years their most important crop. When the weevil would not permit them to raise cotton, they turned to other crops, and soon found that they were more prosperous than ever. They felt so grateful to the boll weevil for having forced them to find a better way of farming that they built a monument to him. The inscription on the monument is as follows:

IN PROFOUND APPRECIATION

OF THE BOLL WEEVIL

AND WHAT IT HAS DONE AS THE HERALD OF PROSPERITY

THIS MONUMENT IS ERECTED

BY THE CITIZENS OF

ENTERPRISE, COFFEE COUNTY, ALABAMA.

BOND PAPER This expression came into use in a perfectly natural manner more than a hundred years ago.

Early in the past century a paper mill was established in Boston, Massachusetts. There was made at this mill an all-rag, hard-surface paper that became popular, especially among those engaged in printing bank notes, bonds, and other legal documents.

By 1853, and possibly earlier, some of those who ordered paper from this mill wrote that they wished some of that superior "bank note paper, or what is sometimes called bond paper."

In time, *bond paper* was used for any good quality paper of a kind suitable for correspondence. But it received its name because it was used in printing bonds.

BOSS   Words appeal to the emotions of people as well as to their intellects. Some words soothe one's feelings, but others arouse dislike or hatred. The first settlers who came to New England were glad that in this new land they were without masters. They despised *master* because it reminded them of a social order they hoped they were through with forever.

They found an excellent way to get along without the word. In Dutch *baas* means "master." The early English settlers in New York borrowed this word in the form of *boss* and used it instead of *master*. It quickly became popular all over the country and is still in everyday use.

It should be noticed, however, that *boss* has never been able to secure anything but colloquial standing in the language. It is quite useful among friends in familiar conversation and writings of an informal sort. When it is used of one in political control of a district or situation it is slang.

BOWERY   In 1661 Peter Stuyvesant, the Dutch governor of what is now New York, purchased from the Dutch West India Company a *bouwerij*, that is, a "farm," situated between the present Fifth and Seventeenth streets and extending from the East River to Fourth Avenue. The governor built a country home on this tract, and around it he grouped homes for the farmers who worked the land.

A road, much of it then through dense forests, connected this little settlement of farmers with the larger settlement to the south known as New Amsterdam. Stuyvesant's country place, with its abundance of shade and footpaths and flowers, became a popular pleasure resort; and the road to it became known after a time as the *Bowery Road*, that is, the road out to the farm. In the course of time this road became part of a street in New York City, but it kept a trace of its ancestry in the name *Bowery*.

BRAIN TRUST   The fact is well-known among scholars that the same word is sometimes coined more than once by clever people who are so widely separated by time and space that they could not have known of each other's existence.

General Hugh Johnson said in 1940 that *brain trust* had been used by Army men as an uncomplimentary term for the first American general staff established by Elihu Root in 1901. There is no reason to doubt General Johnson's statement, but no printed example of the use he remembered has been found. Presumably this *brain trust* has now disappeared entirely.

In 1910, George Fitch, a novelist, used *brain trust* in a *Saturday Evening Post* story. He employed the expression with reference to the faculty of "good old Siwash," the college about which he was writing. The term did not catch on.

Twenty-two years later, during the presidential campaign of 1932, James M. Kieran, a reporter for the *New York Times,* used *Brains Trust* with reference to three Columbia University professors who were helping Franklin D. Roosevelt with his campaign speeches. Some of Mr. Roosevelt's friends did not like the term, but he himself favored it. In the slightly modified form *brain trust* it is still widely used in this country, but it is said that in England *Brains Trust,* or *brains trust,* is preferred.

BRISTLECONE PINE   Nearly a hundred years ago, George Engelmann, a distinguished physician and botanist, found on some of the mountains of the West a pine that had never been called to the attention of scientists.

This pine has little curved, bristlelike prickles about a quarter of an inch long at the end of each of the scales of its small, chocolate-brown cones. Dr. Engelmann accordingly gave the tree the scientific name *Pinus aristata,* that is, "awned or bearded pine." The common name, *bristle-cone pine,* serves pretty well as a translation of the scientific one.

But this pine has other names, such as *cattail pine, foxtail pine.* These allude to the arrangement of the needles in brushlike tufts at the ends of the twigs. Another name for the bristlecone is *jack pine,* a name which denotes inferiority. *Jack pine* is a name for various American pines that are of little importance.

And the bristlecone is clearly inferior. It grows with amazing slowness and seldom reaches forty feet in height. Sometimes a tree that is three or four hundred years old may be as much as thirty inches in diameter. They grow on mountains eight or ten thousand feet above sea level.

Recently, however, a thing was found out about this pine that more than makes up for its unattractive appearance. It is the oldest authentically dated living thing on earth! Formerly it was thought the sequoias (see p. 192), some of them more than three thousand years old, had this distinction; but it is now known that some of the old, ruined, worn out and partially dead bristlecone pines in the White Mountains of California are nearly five thousand years old. Some of those old gnarled, twisted trees on lonely mountain heights and slopes were four or five hundred years old when Abraham walked the earth.

BROADWAY   The first Dutch settlers who came to what is now New York City built Fort Amsterdam on the south end of Manhattan Island. From the fort a road led north to the present city of Albany. For much of the way it followed an old Indian trading path.

Because this road was one of the best they had, the Dutch called it the *Bredeweg*. When the English took possession of New York they translated the name of the road into *Broadway*, for that is what its Dutch name meant. Part of the old road later became a street in New York City, and still has the name *Broadway*. The old route to Albany is still used, too; that is why Broadway is sometimes called the longest street in the world, 150 miles long.

More than fifty years ago Broadway received a nickname in an unusual manner. In December 1901 a new novel appeared with the title *The Great White Way*. The scene of the story was the region of snow and ice around the South Pole. At that time there was a column in a popular New York newspaper telling about things of interest taking place along Broadway. It was the practice of the writer of this column to use at the head of it the title of some current novel. When the novel just mentioned came out, the newspaper writer entitled his column one day: "Found on the Great White Way."

Broadway happened to be covered with snow at the time this issue of the paper appeared. Those who read the column at once associated "The Great White Way" with Broadway, and the title of a novel, now long forgotten, became the nickname of a famous street.

The brilliant illuminations in the theater district on Broadway are often thought to explain the nickname, but they had no part in the origin of it.

BRONX   This word preserves the name of Jonas Bronck, who reached the Dutch settlement in what is now New York City in July, 1639. He came from Holland, but he was a Dane. He purchased five hundred acres of land from the Dutch West India Company, and then, being an honest man, bought it over again from two Indian chiefs who, he felt sure, had a better claim to it than the Dutch.

His five hundred acres of woodlands and meadows and hills lay just north of the place where the Harlem and East rivers join, being east of the Harlem River and west of the stream now known as the Bronx River. He built the first house in this region and named it Emmaus after a village not far from Jerusalem mentioned in the New Testament.

Bronck got along well with the Indians. He dealt honestly with them and they trusted him. In times of Indian troubles, none of his household was ever harmed by the natives.

BUCKEYE   When the first European settlers crossed the Allegheny Mountains and came into what is now Ohio and Kentucky, they found a horse chestnut tree they called *buckeye* because its dark-brown nut looks very much like the eye of a buck deer. The pioneers quickly learned that this tree was of use to them in many ways.

It grows on fertile soil, so its presence was an invitation to those looking for good farm land to stop and settle. Its wood is not difficult to cut, so the firstcomers made bowls, spoons, troughs, and even cradles of it. They planed straight sections of the wood into nice long shavings which they used to make pretty summer hats. Pioneer women found the roots of the buckeye could be used as a soap for washing woolens.

Many people prize the nut of this tree as a good-luck piece. It is fully as useful in this respect as a rabbit's foot, and has the additional advantage, so it is said, of protecting the one who carries it from suffering with rheumatism.

The tree entered so largely into the daily lives of the settlers who first stopped in the region where it is found that the people were soon called *Buckeyes*. This nickname is still used for those who live in Ohio.

CABLEGRAM   Ten years after this now common word was first used in 1868 in New York City, a dictionary which included it condemned it as a low, colloquial term. The reason it was at first looked upon with disfavor is that it is made of parts that come from different languages. *Cable-* is derived from Latin, and *-gram* is of Greek origin.

For more than a century scholars have called words of such mixed ancestry "hybrids." English is liberally supplied with them. Such words as *around, because, brutish, closeness, dentist, falsehood, grateful, princely, parliament, starvation, talkative, ostrich,* and *pedestal* are merely a few samples of words of this kind.

As soon as *cablegram* appeared, a reader of a London

newspaper wrote the editor about the "bad" word and hoped it could be replaced by "calogram," which he explained was much better, being altogether Greek in its make-up. But no one helped this reader with his substitute word, and now few have ever heard of it.

CALLIOPE   A little more than a hundred years ago, Joshua C. Stoddard of Worcester, Massachusetts, began to try to tune steam whistles. He finally succeeded, and secured a patent on a steam organ. In 1856, on the Fourth of July, the city of Worcester and the countryside for miles around were serenaded by the musical steam machine Mr. Stoddard had made. The instrument caused great excitement. People came from far and near to see and admire it. Newspapers described it as a "gigantic novelty blowing a hurricane of music." It was said that this steam organ could be heard twelve miles! One writer reported that two miles was a good distance for hearing it at its best, the notes at that distance being soft and musical and seeming to permeate the entire atmosphere.

No wonder the inventor wanted a fine name for this wonderful organ. He named it a *calliope,* this being the name of the Greek Muse of eloquence and epic poetry. The name of the Muse means "beautiful-voiced," but whether or not a calliope deserves this name is open to doubt. These instruments were formerly used on river steamboats. At present they are sometimes heard at fairs and circuses.

a circus calliope

CALUMET   The most widespread and sacred object used by the North American Indians was a hollow shaft or reed anywhere from eighteen inches to four feet long. Many Indians burned tobacco as a sacrifice to their gods. It occurred to them to provide this hollow shaft or reed with a bowl and use it as a sacrificial altar or pipe.

They ornamented this pipe in many different ways. Feathers from the great bald eagle were often used, for this eagle, living and flying high in the heavens, was thought to be in close touch with the gods whose favor the Indians were anxious to obtain.

When the Indians made a solemn agreement of any kind, they confirmed it by burning tobacco in one of these sacred pipes. Each one present at such a solemn ceremony

took the pipe and drew a whiff of smoke to signify his approval of what had been agreed. The Indians believed any violation of an agreement confirmed in this manner would bring down the wrath of the gods upon the violator.

The French were the first Europeans to become acquainted with the use the Indians made of this highly ornamented and revered object. Since the main part of it was a reed, the French referred to it as a *calumet*, that being their word for a "reed." It was from the French that those who spoke English secured *calumet* in this sense.

CANOE BIRCH   From the Great Lakes region northward, Indians made canoes of the bark of the most widespread birch in the world. It grows well in New England and covers the entire eastern part of Canada. From the use Indians and pioneers made of its bark it is known as *canoe birch*, though it has many other names, such as *paper birch*, *silver birch*, *white birch*.

CAPITOL   Americans were formerly often ridiculed by Europeans for taking perfectly grand names and using them for ridiculously insignificant places. A settlement with only two or three log cabins and perhaps a tavern might be called *London*; two houses in sight of each other and with a swamp between them might be *Rome*.

This tendency on the part of frontiersmen to help themselves to the best names possible accounts for our use of *Capitol* for the building at Washington, D.C., in which Congress meets, and for the house in which the legislature of a state holds its sessions.

In October, 1698, the building in which the governmental affairs of the Virginia colony were carried on burned. The governor and his council decided to transfer the seat of government to a little village known then as Middle Plantation, the present Williamsburg, not far from Jamestown.

They specified that a square of land, 475 feet on a side, should be set aside for the building they planned to erect. And they enacted that "the said building shall forever be called and known by the name of *the Capitol*." Up to this time *Capitol* had never been used in English except as the name of the great national temple at Rome, dedicated to

Jupiter Optimus Maximus (that is, the "Best and Greatest"), the mighty national god of the Romans.

A critic took the governor severely to task for having "graced" this brick house in the wilderness "with the magnificent name of the *Capitol*," but the "magnificent name" has done well in this new use. It has spread over the entire country. It has only one competitor. *Statehouse*, another American coinage, sometimes takes its place when a state Capitol is meant.

CARROUSEL   The simplest form of merry-go-round is a revolving platform so nicely balanced on a central support that children can easily turn it, and jumping on it, enjoy riding for many revolutions before it stops. About 1870, Wilhelm Schneider of Davenport, Iowa, decided he could make a better device of this kind by having it much larger than usual and provided with two platforms instead of one, a stairway in the center connecting them.

Although Mr. Schneider was German, when he secured a patent on his amusement apparatus he used the French word for a merry-go-round and called it a *carrousel*.

Unfortunately for Mr. Schneider, the piece of playground equipment he patented never became popular. Probably it was too heavy and expensive. But the name he gave it was so well liked that it is now often used for any merry-go-round.

CHEWING GUM   There are many American trees which when cut or bruised produce a form of gum.

In the South the sweet gum tree is noted for the clear gum it produces. It is said the Indians chewed such gum and thought the practice was good for their teeth.

One of the first Americans who ever tried to sell chewing gum was John Bacon Curtis (1827-1897) of Maine. He secured some black-spruce gum, prepared it as well as he could, and spent two days in Portland, Maine, trying to sell it without finding a single buyer. But he did not give up, and finally with the help of his father succeeded in getting spruce gum on the market.

The use of chicle, which is still used as the base of chewing gum, is said to have been started in New York about 1870. Chicle is a resin obtained from a tree that grows in tropical America. The first batch of chicle used in this way is said to have been secured from a secretary of the famous Mexican general Santa Anna, who lived for a time on Staten Island.

When chewing gum was much newer than it is now, the following item appeared in a San Francisco paper: "A stranger in this city might at first be led to suppose that the fair Misses of San Francisco used the 'weed' for chewing purposes. But it is not so; it is merely chewing gum. . . . It is an innocent amusement, and splendid training for the jaws. This training is utilized when they become married."

CHRISTMAS SEAL   In December, 1907, Miss Emily Bissell, Secretary of the Delaware Red Cross, was trying to think of some way she could raise three hundred dollars. The money was badly needed to help a local effort to care for eight poor patients suffering from tuberculosis. Suddenly she thought of getting out little ornamental stamps that might be sold for a penny each.

She at once roughed out a design for a stamp. She sketched a half wreath of holly, and in the center of it placed a red cross. She finished it off with "Merry Christmas." A local artist shaped up her design for nothing, and a printer offered to print the stamps at cost and on credit. She secured fifty thousand of them done in bright red on a white background.

On December 9, 1907, a girl in a Red Cross uniform took her place at a table in a corridor of the Wilmington post office to sell the stamps. They were contained in envelopes on which the following little jingle was printed:

Put this stamp, with message bright,
On every Christmas letter;
Help the tuberculosis fight,
And make the new year better.

Sales were disappointing at first, for people did not know what Miss Bissell and her helpers were trying to do, but later when they found out, the sale of stamps went up most encouragingly. Ten times the three hundred dollars so badly needed was raised, many contributions coming from distant states. The following year similar sales were held in thirty-three states, and the movement quickly grew to cover the entire country.

The *Christmas stamps* as they were at first called, were

later named *Christmas seals* at the request of the Post Office Department, because some people confused them with regular postage stamps.

CHRISTMAS TREE   Long before the first settlers came to this country it was customary in Germany to set up at Christmas a little fir or spruce tree and ornament it with candles and other decorations and hang gifts for relatives and friends on its branches. This custom is such an old one in Germany that it is difficult to say when it began. The Germans call such a tree a *Weihnachtsbaum,* that is, "holy-night tree."

When the German settlers in Pennsylvania put up these evergreen trees as they had been accustomed to do at home, some of their English-speaking neighbors were shocked beyond measure. They thought the Germans were worshiping the tree and that they should by all means be forced to stop such a heathen practice.

But when the whole thing was explained and everybody learned that this ceremony was part of the celebration of Christ's birthday, those who spoke English were so delighted with the custom that they took it over themselves and translated the German name of the tree into *Christmas tree.*

The most remarkable Christmas tree in the world is the General Grant tree, which is 267 feet high and over 40 feet in diameter at the base, in King's Canyon National Park, in California. At this magnificent tree a Christmas ceremony was held at noon on Christmas Day, 1925. The occasion was so impressive that the thought occurred to some of those present to call this fine tree the "Nation's Christmas Tree." This was done and each year Christmas services are held there and broadcast throughout the world.

CLAY PIGEON   Sometimes a most commonplace occurrence sets in motion a train of thought in the mind of someone and in time leads to the coining of a term that becomes known all over the world.

Boys are fond of skipping flat stones and shells along the surface of ponds, lakes, and rivers. One day George Ligowsky of Cincinnati, Ohio, saw some boys engaged in this pastime, and the sight gave him an idea. Target shooting was popular then, as it is now. Birds, usually pigeons, were used as targets, but they were becoming more expensive, and public sentiment was against using them in such a cruel manner.

Mr. Ligowsky wondered if he might not be able to make a target of clay that would sail through the air somewhat in the manner of the flat shells and stones he had seen the boys skipping along the surface of the water. He set to work molding such targets. The first ones he made were too hard; they would ring like a bell when they were hit, but they would not break. But the inventor persisted, and by 1881 secured a patent on what he called "flying targets."

Because these first targets were made of clay, and because they usually took the place of pigeons, they were soon called *clay pigeons*. Although they are not and never were shaped like pigeons, and are no longer made of clay, this convenient name for them remains.

COED   In the matter of education, so many new things have been done in this country that there has been need for a number of new terms to indicate the changes that have been made.

One of the first matters to receive the attention of those in authority in the Massachusetts Colony was education. In 1642 they took the new and astonishing step of requiring all parents to provide elementary education for their children, boys and girls alike. In ancient times, it was not thought proper to send girls to school.

But even in this country, for a long time education for girls in high schools and colleges was not as easily obtained as it was for boys. Then in 1834 in the newly established Oberlin College in Ohio the way gradually opened for young women to attend college along with young men. As soon as this step forward had been taken, words such as *coed, coeducate, coeducation, coeducational,* had to be provided.

Coed is an interesting word. It is so short and neat that one instinctively thinks of it as an abbreviation, but it is not. About 1893 when dictionaries first began to record it, they labeled it "College Slang" or "Student Slang," but for at least a quarter of a century they have been leaving off this label, although it is still considered a colloquialism.

When the first coeds finished their college courses and were ready for their degrees, a difficulty about terms arose.

At first it was felt to be improper to call a young woman a "Bachelor of Arts" or a "Doctor of Philosophy," because "bachelor" and "doctor" are masculine words. For a time, therefore, such expressions as *Maid of Arts, Maid of Science, Maid of Philosophy,* were experimented with but quickly given up. Now it no longer seems odd for a young woman to be an A.B. or M.A. or Ph.D. Fortunately it was not necessary for a girl to be called an *alumnus* of a school, for this Latin word was easily provided with the feminine form, *alumna,* which suits a girl admirably.

COMPASS PLANT   When pioneers began to cross the great western Plains, they came upon a remarkable plant the leaves of which always point north and south. Some of those who first saw it called it the *polar plant,* but it is best known as the *compass plant.*

In January, 1847, when Longfellow was writing *Evangeline,* he received a letter from General Benjamin Alvord telling him about this plant. Longfellow was so interested in the plant that he referred to it as follows in his poem:

> Look at this delicate plant that lifts its head
> from the meadow,
> See how the leaves all point to the north, as true
> as the magnet;
> It is the compass flower, that the finger of God
> has suspended
> Here on its fragile stalk, to direct the traveller's
> journey
> Over the sea-like, pathless, limitless waste of
> the desert.

By the time Longfellow's poem was published, the plant was so well-known that a friend told the poet his description of it was not accurate; it is anything but "delicate" or "fragile," having a coarse stem from six to eight feet tall, with leaves a foot or more in length.

Longfellow then corrected this part of his poem by rewriting the lines to read this way:

> Look at this vigorous plant that lifts its head
>   from the meadow,
> See how its leaves are turned to the north, as true
>   as the magnet;
> This is the compass flower, that the finger of God
>   has planted
> Here in the houseless wild, to direct the traveller's
>   journey
> Over the sea-like, pathless, limitless waste of
>   the desert.

The name, *compass flower*, which Longfellow used never became popular. The plant is much too big and hardy to be called a flower.

CONCORD GRAPE   In 1840 Ephraim W. Bull bought a home in Concord, Massachusetts, which is on a river of the same name. One day in the autumn some boys who had been rambling along the river found an abundance of wild grapes. They gathered more than they could eat, and then threw some of them away as they passed Mr. Bull's place.

The following spring a grape plant came up on Mr. Bull's land, and he tended it carefully. It did well and by 1843 bore fruit. Mr. Bull took the best bunch of grapes he could find on the little vine, and planted the seeds. By 1849 the new plants bore grapes. He tested all of them and saved only the best for replanting.

He named this fine fruit *Concord grape*, and within a few years it became widely cultivated under this name. Its hardiness, productivity, and freedom from disease caused it to become the most widely grown grape in the eastern part of our country.

CONESTOGA WAGON   There is no doubt that *Conestoga* is of Indian origin. The Conestoga Indians lived in the valley of the Susquehanna River at the head of Chesapeake Bay. Some scholars think their name meant "roily or muddy water" and alluded to the river along which they lived.

In colonial days German settlers made homes in the Conestoga region of Pennsylvania. Among them were expert wagonmakers. They found excellent wood there and were soon busy making what were known as *Conestoga wagons,* the most famous farm-and-freight vehicles of their day. They were so well-known that as early as 1750 one of the best inns in Philadelphia was known as the Conestoga Wagon.

As soon as the Cumberland Road was opened, hundreds of these wagons began to appear on it loaded with freight for the frontier settlements beyond the mountains. Because these wagons had white canvas covers to protect their loads in case of bad weather they were called *covered wagons*, an expression which may have been first used with reference to these wagons.

Often drawn by as many as six large Conestoga horses, these big, heavily loaded wagons went slowly, three or four miles an hour, over the long turnpike. The drivers whiled away the long hours as best they could, often

smoking as they looked out over the wild countryside through which they were passing.

Some enterprising American had the idea of making an unusually long, cheap cigar which he thought would appeal especially to these wagoners. His long, slim cigars sold for a cent a piece and were so popular with the Conestoga freighters that they soon became known as *Conestoga cigars*.

Soon this name underwent shortening, and such a cigar became known as a *stogie*, or *stogy*. Long, slender cigars called *stogies* are still on the market.

CONGRESSIONAL   A century and a half ago many people, both in the United States and in England, were alarmed because Americans were adding words to the language. They thought the English language belonged to those who lived in Great Britain, and that Americans should show their appreciation of being allowed to use it by not making any changes in it.

Noah Webster was too intelligent to think any such foolish thing as this. On June 4, 1800, he announced that he was going to make a dictionary of the American language. He said: "New circumstances, new modes of life, new ideas of various kinds, give rise to new words, and have already made many material differences between the language of England and America."

This plain statement of a simple truth greatly alarmed those who felt that Webster and others who thought as he did "would unsettle the whole of our admirable language." A former tutor at Yale, when he learned what Webster proposed to do, was so indignant that he wrote: "Let, then, the projected volume of *foul* and *unclean* things bear his own Christian name and be called NOAH'S ARK."

When Webster's dictionary appeared in 1806 it was at once examined closely for such "foul and unclean" words as "wicked" Americans had been adding to the language. One critic was outraged when he came upon *Congressional* and *Presidential,* neither of which had ever before appeared in a dictionary. He denounced them as "barbarous terms," and said they were "equally unnecessary, and offensive to the ear."

Ten years later, however, one of the best educated men in the United States announced with pleasure that an English friend had written him that "the term *Congress* belonging to America, the Americans may employ its derivatives, without waiting for the assent of the English."

This gracious news was most comforting to those who felt that Americans should not make any new words unless the English permitted them to do so.

CONTINENTAL, *not worth a continental*
When the Revolutionary War began, the Continental Congress in Philadelphia had to secure money to carry on the struggle.

There was no source from which money in large sums could be borrowed, so Congress issued paper money in the form of bills. The members of the Congress voted the first issue of 2 million dollars on June 22, 1775. By November, 1779, they had approved issues amounting to nearly 250 million dollars.

This "Continental currency," as it was called, soon began to decline in value. Public confidence in the American cause was weak. By January 1781 the money had declined in value so much that it required one hundred dollars of it to equal in value one dollar in silver. By the summer of that year such money was worth even less.

Under these circumstances the expression *not worth a continental* arose and has been in use ever since. The worthlessness of this currency is also alluded to in other expressions such as *not to care a continental.*

COON   The colonists at Jamestown soon found that in the forests around them there lived a useful fur-bearing animal unlike any they had ever seen in England. When they asked the Indians what they called this crea-ture, the natives said something which sounded to the colonists like "arocoun" or "aroughcun." Imitating the na-tives as best they could, the settlers called the animal in question a *raccoon,* a name which after a time became shortened to *coon.*

The thing about this animal which impressed the In-dians most was that his forepaws look very much like tiny hands. With these little hands he gets a good deal of his food by scratching in moist ground along branches and creeks for earthworms, crawfish, and turtle eggs. He also likes mice and often scratches them out of their shal-low burrows. So the Indians gave him a name which means "he scratches with his hands."

COWBIRD   There is an American bird that spends a good deal of its time perched on the backs of cows. Because of this it has been given various names that allude to its choice of companions. It is called *cowbird, cow blackbird, cow bunting, cowpen bird,* and *oxbiter.*

This bird is clever enough to make most of its living by being with these much larger animals. It enjoys going over its huge friends and picking off such ticks and other insect pests as it finds.

Then, too, as cattle graze along they stir up various bugs, grasshoppers, and flies that scatter in all directions to get out of the way of the huge beasts. The bird swoops down on such of these fleeing insects as it likes and gets many good meals with the help of its big friends.

This impudent bird carries its cleverness one step too far, however. It does not build a nest, but lays its eggs in the nests of more industrious birds, who unwittingly hatch and raise its young. It is thus fully entitled to the name *lazybird*, which is sometimes given it.

COWCATCHER   When people in this country first began building railroads, they often made them through miles and miles of uncleared and unsettled forests. It was the custom in those days for farmers to allow their hogs, cattle, sheep, and, sometimes, horses to go at large in the woods. Frequently these creatures got on the railroad tracks and, in addition to losing their lives, caused wrecks.

Something had to be done about these accidents, so about 1830 a young man named Isaac Dripps mounted two heavy iron spears on a small truck, which he then placed just ahead of the locomotive. This device was not at all satisfactory, because it was fatal to the animals it struck.

Finally a strong sloping frame—at least ten feet long— was made and fastened to the front of the locomotive. It shielded the wheels and at the same time pushed aside or scooped up cattle, sheep, and other obstructions from the track.

A name was needed for this contrivance, which as time went on was modified and improved. *Guard* was a popular name because the thing's main purpose was to protect the wheels of the locomotive from being thrown off the track. Other names were *cow-lifter, pilot, cowcatcher.* The last name won the day, because it is easy to say.

COYOTE   Many people feel that it is particularly suitable for an American animal to have the name which the natives gave it before white people came here. The coyote has such a name.

The first Europeans to make its acquaintance were Spaniards. When they came upon this doglike prairie wolf in Mexico they asked the Indians what they called it. The Aztecs said their name for the creature was *coyotl.* The Spaniards took over this name in the form *coyote,* and later those who spoke English borrowed it from them.

CRACKER   Words are constantly coming into and going out of all living languages. Similarly, meanings of words are always coming in and fading out. Sometimes this ebb and flow of meanings results in perplexity for students of words.

For example, *cracker* has been used for about two hundred years as a contemptuous nickname for a very poor, unambitious, shiftless white person living in the more backward parts of the South. After this nickname had been in use for a long time, students began to wonder how it arose. Many guesses were made, but for a long time nobody came upon the proper explanation of the term.

At last a student was lucky enough to find the solution of the puzzle in an old letter of June 27, 1766, written in this country to a British official in England. The writer of this letter, in telling about the recent arrest of three troublemakers on the frontier of Georgia, mentioned that they were called *Crackers*. Farther on in his letter he explained how this nickname came to be given them.

> "I should explain to your Lordship what is meant by Crackers; a name they have got from being great boasters; they are a lawless set of rascalls on the frontiers of Virginia, Maryland, the Carolinas, and Georgia. . . . Some of them stay in the Indian country and are perpetually endeavouring to stir up a war by propagating idle stories that they may join them and share in the plunder."

A study of the word *cracker* shows that its meaning, "boaster, bragger, liar," passed out of currency not long after it was first applied to these frontier outlaws. By the time investigators became curious about the origin of the word as a contemptuous nickname, they had no clue to guide them to a proper explanation of it.

CROSSWORD PUZZLE   About a century ago what were known as "word squares" were popular. Such a device is a group of words so selected that when they are written under each other they form a square and may be read either across or down. Here are some examples:

SATED	HEART	CIRCLE
ATONE	EMBER	ICARUS
TOAST	ABUSE	RAREST
ENSUE	RESIN	CREATE
DETER	TREND	LUSTRE
		ESTEEM

In 1913 the *New York World* issued a Sunday supplement entitled FUN. This addition to the paper was a very small section of eight pages, hardly more than 9 x 10 inches in size. It contained jokes, tricks, puzzles, and other simple forms of entertainment.

There was working for the *World* at that time a man named Arthur Wynn, or Winn, and in the December 21, 1913, issue of FUN he presented what was called "FUN'S Word-Cross Puzzle." It is said that he thought of making a puzzle of this kind from having enjoyed word squares when he was a child in England.

The device proved popular, and other puzzles of the same kind appeared regularly in later issues of FUN. Within a few weeks "Word-Cross Puzzle" was rearranged into "Cross-Word Puzzle."

Since then there have been many variations introduced into such puzzles. The first one to appear in FUN is reproduced on the next page. Can you work it?

CROW, *to eat crow*   When anyone has to admit that he was wrong, and do something he had previously said he would never do, he is said *to eat crow, to eat boiled crow,* or *to take a dish of crow.*

FUN'S Word-Cross Puzzle.

FILL in the small squares with words which agree with the following definitions:

2–3. What bargain hunters enjoy.

4–5. A written acknowledgment.

6–7. Such and nothing more.

10–11. A bird.

14–15. Opposed to less.

18–19. What this puzzle is.

22–23. An animal of prey.

26–27. The close of a day.

28–29. To elude.

30–31. The plural of is.

8–9. To cultivate.

12–13. A bar of wood or iron.

16–17. What artists learn to do.

20–21. Fastened.

24–25. Found on the seashore.

10–18. The fibre of the gomuti palm.

6–22. What we all should be.

4–26. A day dream.

2–11. A talon.

19–28. A pigeon.

F–7. Part of your head.

23–30. A river in Russia.

1–32. To govern.

33–34. An aromatic plant.

N–8. A fist.

24–31. To agree with.

3–12. Part of a ship.

20–29. One.

5–27. Exchanging.

9–25. To sink in mud.

13–21. A boy.

The origin of this expression about eating a crow has never been found out. Under such circumstances anyone is free to invent a suitable story to account for what can not be really explained. One of the most amusing stories called forth by this expression is that there was once a boardinghouse keeper whose patrons often complained about the food. The proprietor tried to make light of these complaints and assured his boarders that he was able to eat anything. He said he could even eat a crow.

Some of the boarders decided to put the proprietor to the test. They killed a crow and baked it nicely, but secretly made it as hot as they could with pepper and loaded it with salt. Then they liberally sprinkled it with Scotch snuff.

This tasty-looking dish was set before the proprietor and he was invited to make good on his boast that he could eat crow. He proceeded at once to demonstrate his ability by taking a good bite and chewing away on it. The stuff was far more terrible than he had thought possible, so after struggling as long as he could with the helping they had given him, he shoved back his plate and said, "Yes, I kin eat a crow, but I'll be darned if I hanker after it."

Other explanations have been given of the origin of the expression, but this one appeared in 1851, and is thus entitled to consideration even though it may not be true at all.

CUMBERLAND ROAD It is difficult to realize how difficult transportation was 150 years ago. On

December 3, 1803, a firm in Providence, Rhode Island, sent some yarn to a customer living sixty miles away. In writing him that his order was on the way, the company wrote that he could expect to receive it in "the course of the winter."

In the early days of our country, many people did not think the central government had the right under the Constitution to engage in road building. They thought this was spending the money of all the people to benefit the few who lived near the road.

But there were those who took a different view of the matter, and in 1811 the Federal Government undertook to build a road that would connect the "far western" country in Ohio with Washington, D.C., on the Potomac. At that time there was a canal from Washington to Cumberland, Maryland, so the Government road began at Cumberland. It passed through Uniontown, Pennsylvania, and on west to Wheeling, West Virginia, and later to Zanesville, Ohio. It finally reached Vandalia in Illinois.

This *Cumberland Road,* as it was called, was the main highway of traffic across the Allegheny Mountains in the first quarter of the nineteenth century. It was also known as the *National Road,* or *National Turnpike.* The present U.S. Highway No. 40 follows this old road in many places.

DEMORALIZE   Fortunately, we know who made this term and the occasion upon which he first used it. Noah Webster, the famous dictionary maker, coined *demoralize.* Although he spent fifty years of his life studying words and defining them in dictionaries, this is the only one he ever made. In 1794 he wrote about the French Revolution, and in this he emphasized the bad effects of war, especially civil war, on the morals of the people involved. He referred to these effects as *demoralizing*.

Webster knew he had added a word to the language. He watched to see if others would adopt it, and was pleased to see that the term soon became popular. Before he died in 1843 he knew *demoralize* had become firmly established in the language.

His word has had an unusual thing happen to it. As soon as people began to notice the term, some of them supposed Webster had borrowed it from the French word *démoraliser*, but in a dictionary he brought out in 1828 Webster explained he had made it by placing the common prefix *de-* on *moralize* or *moral*. And this explanation he stuck to as long as he lived.

Not long after his death, however, his word was explained as being derived from French, and some dictionaries still give this explanation of it. How does your dictionary say *demoralize* originated?

DESERET   This word is not often used now, but it came near being quite well known.

It was added to the language in 1830 by Joseph Smith, the founder of the Mormon Church. As he used it, *Deseret* meant honeybee. The Mormons liked it so much that when they settled what is now Utah they hoped the name of their state could be *Deseret*. But Congress did not like the word as a state name. It suggests "desert," which is not a complimentary name to give a state.

Congress found a good substitute for *Deseret* in *Utah*. As early as 1720 Spaniards in the West had written the name of a tribe of Indians in that region *Yutta*. Americans had taken this word up and after spelling it various ways —*Ute, Uta, Utah*—had finally settled on *Utah*. This name was objected to vigorously, especially by those Mormons who were well acquainted with the Indians in question.

The objectors pointed out that at least some of the Indians of that name were a disgrace, for they were dirty and lice-ridden and ate grasshoppers.

But Congress had its way, and instead of admitting the state of *Deseret* into the Union, it created the Territory of Utah in 1850, and later, when the population of the region justified it, admitted the present state into the Union. There were many among the settlers who protested the undemocratic way in which the name *Utah* was forced upon them, but they accepted the decision with good grace and soon forgot having favored *Deseret* at first.

DESERET ALPHABET   The purpose of an alphabet is to supply a sign or symbol, that is, a "letter" for each sound in the language. The English alphabet is by no means perfect, because it has only twenty-six letters to represent the approximately forty-three sounds in the language. If we had a perfect alphabet—one in which each letter stood for one sound—learning to read and spell would be far easier.

When Mormons first settled in Utah, and members of their church from all over Europe began to join them in the settlement, there arose an urgent need for these newcomers to learn English. The idea occurred to some of the leaders in the church to prepare an alphabet that would have a letter for each sound, and thus enable these newcomers to learn English quickly. This alphabet was known as the *Deseret alphabet*.

The effort to make it popular did not succeed, and when Brigham Young died in 1877, the use of it was given up. He had been greatly interested in the undertaking, and had done all he could to make it a success.

DIXIE   It is too bad that this well-known and rather pretty name for the Southern states cannot be explained in a satisfactory manner. Many explanations have been given, and those who come upon one of them often think it is the only one and accept it as quite correct.

Probably the most popular explanation is this one: Before the Civil War there was a bank in Louisiana that issued ten-dollar notes. French was and still is used in parts of Louisiana, so these notes had on one side a large *dix,* the French word meaning "ten." According to this theory, that part of the state, and finally all the South, became known as the "land of the Dixes or Dixies," and finally *Dixie.*

The trouble with this explanation is that positive proof for it is lacking. No one has so far found any example of "land of the Dixes" used for the South.

DOPE   This is one of the words that has been borrowed into American English from the language of the Dutch settlers in New York. In Dutch *doop* means "sauce." The English-speaking neighbors of the Dutch enjoyed the sauce, and borrowed the word, which they spelled *dope.* At first they used their newly borrowed word in the sense of gravy, but it now has many meanings.

Although it has been in the English language for a century and a half, *dope* has had the misfortune of being chiefly slang. Even the expressions formed with it, such as *dope book, dope bucket, dope fiend, dope peddler, dope ring, dope sheet, fly dope,* have only slang standing. Terms derived from it, such as *dopester* and *dopey,* are likewise slang, and their use is to be avoided in formal writing and speaking.

There is nothing about *dope* itself to explain why it should have such a poor standing. Its close relatives— *deep, dimple, dip, dive*—are quite respectable. Poor old *dope* is just the black sheep in a family of respectable and well-thought-of words, and there is nothing anyone can do about it.

DUCK STAMP   This is such a new term that dictionaries do not have it. It has been appearing in the newspapers for a few years, however, and seems likely to remain in the language for a long time.

The need for it arose in 1934 when Congress passed the Migratory Hunting Stamp Act. At that time, sportsmen and others interested in protecting water birds were afraid all of them were going to be killed just as the passenger pigeons had been. Money was needed to enable the Fish and Wildlife Service of the Government to protect these water birds better. The law of 1934 provided for raising money by the sale of migratory bird-hunting stamps.

Every year stamps with new designs are brought out and sent to about seventeen thousand post offices where they go on sale July 1. Those who wish to hunt ducks have to purchase them, so they refer to them as *duck stamps.*

EGG BEATER   Eggs may be beaten with many things. If nothing better is at hand, a spoon or fork will do. In early times someone in England thought of using a small bundle of wires called a *whisk,* or *egg whisk.* This turned out to be a fairly good implement for the purpose.

In pioneer times in this country, merchants often had small wooden hickory rods to sell to those who needed something with which to beat eggs. They served rather well, because the wood of the hickory is tough and entirely free of any odor or gum that might spoil the flavor of the eggs. The first egg beater of the type now familiar was put on the market about 1866 by the Dover Stamping Company of Dover, New Hampshire. It worked by hand, of course, and was a simple arrangement of two cogged wheels which, when turned, whirled the whisklike beaters round and round.

The company at once secured the use of *Dover* as a trade-mark and patented their beater. It is still often called a *Dover egg beater*.

ELECTROCUTE   Sometimes words become involved in popularity contests with others, and for a time it is doubtful which of them will survive. *Electrocute* won in a contest of this kind.

About 1875 Thomas A. Edison and George Westinghouse became interested in using electric current to light up homes and even entire cities. As soon as they began

to try to harness electricity, they found it was more dangerous than people had thought. Accidents were distressingly common. Many workmen lost their lives.

At that time there was not in the language any word meaning "to put to death by electricity." Such a word was obviously needed, and many people suggested terms they thought might be suitable. The race finally narrowed down to two words very much alike—*electricute* and *electrocute.* Educated people favored *electricute* because both parts of it, *electri-* and *-cute,* are from the same language, Latin. *Electrocute,* they thought, would not do, for its first part, *electro-,* is Greek, and to join a Greek element with a Latin one is regarded by scholars as a bad thing to do.

The contest between the two terms went on for a long time. *Electricute* was preferred in a large dictionary which appeared about 1895, and it was hoped this would help its chances to win. But it did not help enough, for after a time it became obvious that most people were using *electrocute.* Not many people care whether a word has Greek and Latin elements mixed in it.

So *electrocute* won the contest, no matter what the scholars thought. In the large unabridged Webster's dictionary, however, the following note appears after this popularity-winning term:

> *Electrocute* has been considered by many to be inelegant, but is widely used and has no accepted equivalent.

ENGLISH SPARROW   It seems to be the rule that birds having the fewest desirable ways and habits are the ones most easily introduced from one country into another.

In this country there is a caterpillar pest known as a *measuring worm,* though other names, such as *inchworm, spanworm,* are also used for it. In 1850 the thought occurred to someone to try to get rid of these caterpillars by bringing into this country a widespread and well-known European sparrow. Eight pairs were brought to Brooklyn, New York, and liberated. Others were brought later, and they thrived wherever they were carried. The result has been that these pesky sparrows are now found over nearly all of the United States. The name most often used for them is *English sparrow* because the first ones were brought here from England.

No doubt they have destroyed many measuring worms, but they have by no means vanquished all of them. They are not popular with other birds or with people. Their filthy habits and destructive ways (they eat grain and tree buds) have caused them to be compared often with rats.

ESCALATOR   At the Paris Exposition in 1900 there was a remarkable exhibition of a moving stairway. This invention did away with the bother of climbing stairs. All one had to do to go upstairs was to step on a moving tread at the foot of the stairs and be carried smoothly and safely to the floor above.

This exhibit had been sent over by the Otis Elevator Company of New York City. It was brought back to this country after the exposition was over and installed in a large store in Philadelphia. Soon thousands of people had ridden on this wonderful contrivance and learned that it was called an *Escalator*.

Dictionaries had to take account of this new word. Scholars at first were puzzled over its make-up. A long and learned, but quite erroneous, explanation of it as being from an imaginary French word *escalateur* appeared in a dictionary that came out in 1909.

Escalator was coined as a trade-mark for the Otis Elevator Company. It was cleverly made in the form of a Latin word. It has the prefix *e-* often found in Latin words such as those from which we get *elide, eliminate, elude, emend, emerge,* and many more. Then comes the Latin word *scala,* meaning ladder, and then the ending *-tor* found in many Latin words such as *administrator, agitator, creator, dictator, gladiator, imitator, legislator, spectator*—to mention only a few of those that have in English the same forms they had in Latin.

Dictionaries in calling *Escalator* a modern Latin word allude to the fact that it has the form of a Latin term.

FEDORA   In 1882 a French dramatist wrote a play for Sarah Bernhardt, the most celebrated French actress of that time. The leading role in the play was Fedora Romanoff, a Russian princess, and the play took its name, *Fédora,* from her. The play was so popular that it reached London the next year, and then came to America. It opened at the Fourteenth Street Theater in New York on

October 1, 1884, with Fanny Davenport as the star and Robert B. Mantell as leading man.

The play was a great success. Fanny Davenport as Fedora delighted the thousands who saw her. Her popularity spread the name throughout the country. An enterprising hat manufacturer named one of his hats a *Fedora* to take advantage of the popular enthusiasm. And the name lives on now in the speech of thousands who never heard of Fanny Davenport or of the Russian princess whose part she played.

Fedora is a name worthy of a princess. It is the Russian feminine form of *Fëdor*, a shortened form of *Feodor*, the Russian equivalent of *Theodore*, which means "gift of God." It is almost too beautiful to use for a hat!

FERRIS WHEEL   A few years before the Chicago Exposition opened in 1893, there had been a similar one held in Paris. For this fair a French engineer, A. G. Eiffel, had designed an iron tower 984.25 feet high that had attracted world-wide wonder and admiration.

Those in charge of preparations at Chicago hoped to do something that would rival the Eiffel Tower.

Only a few months before the exposition was to open, George Washington Gale Ferris, an American engineer, had an idea. He would build an enormous wheel, 250 feet in diameter, which would revolve on a great central axis and carry cars for passengers on its rim. He lost no time in completing the drawings for this huge novelty. His plans were approved and work began at once. In the remarkably short time of six months the wheel was ready for use.

It was a wonderful thing indeed. The axle was 45 feet long and 32 inches in diameter. It weighed 70 tons, and rested on secure supports 140 feet from the ground. There were 36 cars around the great wheel's outer edge and these were capable of carrying 1,440 passengers. As the wheel slowly turned on its great axle it lifted the passengers 270 feet above the exposition grounds, giving them a wonderful view of all the surrounding country.

The wheel was such an attraction that about 92 per cent of those who attended the exposition rode on it. They spread its name, *Ferris wheel,* to all parts of the world.

FLICKER   All over the eastern half of North America there lives a handsome good-natured bird that never grows weary of making his presence known to everybody in hearing distance. His notes have caused different names to be given him.

Most people call him a *flicker* because he says *flicker,*

flecker, flika, flitter, or something that sounds like one of these words. Others think *flicker* comes from his habit of winging his way along in a wavy, up-and-down flight, from ten to a hundred feet from the ground.

To some people he seems to be saying *harri-wicket,* or *harrow-wicket,* or *herri-wicket,* and they are inclined to call him *Harry-Wicket* or to shorten this and call him simply *wicket.*

Others have given him names that allude to the bright-yellow undersides of his wings. *Golden-winged woodpecker* is a good name for him and one often used. *Yellowhammer* is a suitable name also, for there is a great deal of yellow in his appearance, and he is usually busy hammering away at something with his long, strong bill.

He is such a large, handsome fellow with a form that resembles that of a pigeon that he is sometimes called *pigeon woodpecker* or *wood pigeon.*

No matter what people call him, he is popular with other birds. He appears to enjoy their admiration of him, and likes robins and bluebirds especially. He even gets on well with English sparrows and hawks.

FRANKLIN'S GULL   This name is derived from that of Sir John Franklin, a celebrated English navigator and explorer. The beautiful bird known by it is also called *prairie pigeon,* and *Franklin's rosy gull.*

It is the only bird in the United States to have a monument named for it in grateful recollection of its service to humanity. For it was this bird that rescued early settlers in the Salt Lake region from the terrible Mormon cricket (see p. 150) that was devastating their wheat in the spring of 1848. This battle was one of the most desperate ever fought on this continent. A huge army of these handsome gulls took an eager part in the engagement, and with their help the first settlers in Utah won a victory which saved them from starvation.

When Utah became a state the legislature passed a law forbidding anyone to harm one of these fine birds. And the grateful citizens erected a beautiful monument to express their thanks to God for sending these birds to their help. The monument shows the gulls sweeping in to help the first settlers, and is called "The Sea Gull Monument."

GHOST TOWN   It is surprising that *ghost town* did not originate sooner than it did, for certainly old, abandoned cities in other parts of the world must have often made those looking over their ruins think of ghosts. But *ghost town* is a new term, hardly fifty years old.

It came into use in connection with western towns that were settled quickly in early times and then soon abandoned. Most of them sprang up in regions where gold or silver deposits had been found. They prospered as long as mining was profitable, but when the mineral deposits were exhausted and there was nothing left to support the places, those who had lived there moved off to seek fortunes elsewhere.

Not all ghost towns were once the scenes of mining activities. Towns situated where it was hoped a railroad was

going to be often became ghost towns when the railroad changed its course and the town turned out to be miles away from where the road was actually built.

G-MAN   Sometimes a word appears suddenly under dramatic circumstances that cause it to become widely used and to remain in the language.

On September 26, 1933, agents of the division now known as the Federal Bureau of Investigation trapped a notorious criminal, George Kelly, in one of his hide-outs in Memphis, Tennessee. Waiting for them with a drawn gun, he suddenly decided to surrender as they closed in on him, and shouted, "Don't shoot, G-men, don't shoot."

From the criminal's use of it, *G-man* became well-known overnight. The Federal agents said it was the first time anyone had ever used that name for them. Some of those interested in the expression said it was an underworld term meaning "Government man," and had only recently come into use.

Scholars have not been able so far to find out all they

would like to know about the expression, but they have learned that it was used as early as 1916 in Ireland to refer to a detective of the British Government. How much earlier it may have been employed, and in just what sense, is not at present known.

GOPHER   This word is used of two animals that are as unlike as two creatures can well be. When a situation of this kind exists, scholars suspect that two words have become merged into one. The correct explanation of *gopher* appears to be as follows.

In early times in the South, the land tortoise found there was known as a *magofer*. The source of this name can not be made out. Possibly it comes from some Indian word. It soon went out of use, and in its place *gopher* appeared. It looks very much as if *magofer* was shortened and the latter part of it, *gofer,* was used alone. This would account for the name of the land tortoise.

The French who were the first to settle in what is now Louisiana found there a little burrowing rodent or ground squirrel common in the prairie regions of that state and throughout the western and some of the northern states. These little animals live in colonies, and they dig so many holes or burrows that to the French the ground reminded them of what they called *gaufre,* that is, "honeycomb." It is thought that their word for honeycomb became in English *gopher* and was soon applied to the little creature that did the honeycombing.

The land tortoise, or gopher, found in the South has a

shell about twelve inches long and ten inches wide. He is an independent fellow, and with his strong front feet digs out a home for himself away from any of his kind. He never "honeycombs" the ground as the much smaller gopher of the prairie regions is fond of doing.

GORILLA   This word came into the English language at Boston, Massachusetts, in 1847.

Eight or nine hundred years before the birth of Christ, a great city, Carthage, was founded in northern Africa. About 500 B.C. Hanno, an admiral of that city, sailed west on an exploring expedition. When he passed through the Straits of Gibraltar, he turned south and sailed along the coast of Africa. He secured some natives to be interpreters for him as he sailed further south skirting the coast.

One day his men went ashore and found a number of strange, hairy, manlike apes or beasts of some kind. With great difficulty the sailors captured three and tried to carry them away, but they struggled so fiercely the sailors killed them and took along only their skins. The sailors asked the interpreters the name of these ferocious creatures, and they told them they were *gorillas*.

When the expedition returned to Carthage, a written account of the voyage was placed on the walls of one of the temples in that great city. While it was there, someone who spoke Greek came along and read it. It was not very long, so this passer-by copied it. Formerly when Greek was studied more than it is now, this account was often read by students in school.

Many centuries later an American missionary, T. S. Savage, went to Africa. While there he learned that in parts of that country there are large terrible apes. He was a scientist as well as a missionary and made a study of these ferocious creatures. He prepared an interesting paper about them, and in 1847 read it before a natural history society in Boston. In this paper he suggested that these creatures be called *gorillas*, the name African interpreters had used for the fierce creatures Hanno's sailors had come upon centuries before.

GRAHAM FLOUR   Sylvester Graham was born in West Suffield, Connecticut, in 1794. He became a minister and at the same time took great interest in diet and physiology. He soon began to give talks on health and diet. He found people were much more interested in these discussions than they were in his sermons.

Some of his ideas about food amused those who heard him. He advised the eating of vegetables, and homemade bread at least twelve hours old, made of coarsely ground flour that had not been sifted.

His views about food aroused a great deal of controversy. His system of diet was called *Grahamism*, and those who approved it were *Grahamites*—terms not used as much now as they were formerly. Many jokes were made about him and his ideas. Ralph Waldo Emerson called him the "poet of bran meal and pumpkins."

But as a result of his teachings there are now in the language such terms as *graham flour, graham cracker, graham biscuit, graham muffin.* And his name has become so thoroughly a part of the language that it is no longer written with a capital letter in such expressions as these.

GRANDFATHER'S   (or GRANDFATHER) CLOCK   The number of words that have been brought into the English language by songs must be small, but at least there is one such term.

Henry Clay Work was a popular song writer, but only one of the many successful songs he wrote added a term to the language. About 1875 he wrote "Grandfather's Clock," the first stanza of which was:

> My grandfather's clock was too large for the shelf,
>   So it stood ninety years on the floor;
> It was taller by half than the old man himself,
>   Though it weighed not a pennyweight more.
> It was bought on the morn of the day that he was born
>   And was always his treasure and pride.
> But it stopped short—never to go again—
>   When the old man died.

This song was so popular that at least 800,000 copies of it were sold, earning for the composer four thousand dollars, a great sum at that time. And though the author may never have known it, the song added *grandfather's clock* to the English language.

GRIZZLY BEAR   This name is a little puzzling. It was first used about 150 years ago. It has been thought that *grizzly* is a misunderstanding of *grisly* meaning "horrible, terrible," and that the creature was originally called *grisly bear* because the Indians and the white hunters had learned how dangerous he was.

But the best explanation is that *grizzly* has reference to the grayish color of some of these bears. The earliest white men to write about them described different ones they saw as being grizzly, gray, white, and brown. *Grizzly* is the most popular name of this famous bear, and has been used in about two hundred place names in California as *Grizzly Bluff, Grizzly Flats, Grizzly Mountain, Grizzly Camp.*

In winter the standard color of a grizzly's coat is brown next to the skin, but the tips of the hairs are silvery gray. From this fact he is often referred to as *silvertip*. In early times some pioneers thought this bear was especially fond of eating mules, so they called him *mule bear*. His huge tracks look somewhat like those of a man wearing moccasins, so another early term for him was *Moccasin Joe*. He is such a fierce fighter that frontiersmen sometimes called him *Caleb*, or *Ephraim*, these being names of great fighters told about in the Bible.

Although grizzlies are no longer found in California, the Indians in the Yosemite region in former times were well acquainted with them. They called these great beasts *u-zú-mai-ti, Jusmites,* or *Josmites,* meaning "the killers." Through an unusual circumstance this name has been preserved in the well-known term *Yosemite* (see p. 235).

GROUND HOG   This name is a misnomer; the little animal that bears it does not in the least resemble a hog. His other common name, *woodchuck*, which is derived from one the Indians gave him, suits him better.

As for the old idea that he is a weather prophet, the explanation is much easier. Long ago there arose a folk belief in Europe that the weather on February 2 shows whether winter is over or not. In different parts of England there are old rimes based on the importance of weather on this day, Candlemas Day as they call it:

> If Candlemas Day be fair and bright,
> Winter will have another flight,
> But if Candlemas Day brings clouds and rain,
> Winter is gone and won't come again.

> On Candlemas-day if the sun shines clear
> The shepherd had rather see his wife on the bier.

> If Candlemas-day be fine and clear
> Corn and fruits will then be dear.

In Germany there was a belief among the common people that on February 2 the badger indicated the nature of the approaching weather by coming out of his winter quarters and looking about to find if he could see his shadow. If he could, he knew at once that winter was not yet over and returned to his den to sleep for another six weeks.

German settlers who came to this country, not having their faithful badger to indicate for them what the weather was going to be, put the ground hog in his place, and told the same story about his activities on February 2 that they were familiar with at home about the badger. *Ground-hog day* has been in the language for at least a century.

HATCHET, *to bury the hatchet*   Indians were greatly impressed by symbols and ceremonies. Among them the tomahawk, or the hatchet, as white people often called it, had many uses both in peace and in war. When an Indian council met to deliberate about war, they might have in a conspicuous place a tomahawk ornamented with feathers and painted blood-red.

If the council concluded that war should be begun, the leader of the young warriors might take up the tomahawk, and holding it in his hand, sing war songs and dance. Then the hatchet would be sent to every tribe concerned. The messenger, having given suitable presents, would throw the hatchet on the ground and if the tribal council agreed to wage war, one of their expert warriors would take it up.

When peace was concluded, a ceremony was held and an Indian hatchet was solemnly buried as a symbol that there would be no more bloodshed. White settlers knew of this custom on the part of the Indians and often joined them in observing it. From this ceremony the expression *to bury the hatchet* has come to mean to make peace and become friends.

HAYWIRE, *to go haywire*   For more than fifty years hay has been put up in compact rectangular bales and securely bound with smooth iron wire which in this country received the name *haywire*.

Before a bundle of hay can be used, the wire around it

must be removed. Careful farmers do not throw this wire away, for it often comes in handy. Usually it is hung up on a nail or hook, and in the course of time quite a mass of it may accumulate.

When a piece of it is needed, the farmer frequently finds that somehow the piece he fancies is so entangled with all the other pieces that it is most exasperating to get it out. Under such circumstances an impatient farmer may use language of a kind he does not ordinarily employ.

Out of this kind of situation the expression *to go haywire* has arisen. It is used in speaking of anyone or anything that is in a state of confusion or disorder or hopelessly mixed up. It is not a dignified expression, but it is quite colorful to those who know how it originated.

HEADLIGHT   This word became a part of the English language in the United States about a hundred years ago. In the earliest days of railroading, trains ran only during the day. When night trains were first operated, there was no way of illuminating the track ahead of them. If a cow or horse happened to be on the track, or if a tree had fallen across it, there was no way of seeing the obstruction in time to avoid an accident.

One of the first attempts to remedy this situation was made by Horatio Allen, a popular railroad engineer. His idea was to attach a small car to the front of the locomotive, and then cover the car with a heavy layer of sand on which a bright bonfire of pine knots was kept burning. This method was not a success. There was plenty of light to be sure, but it was not focused on the tracks; most of it was entirely wasted so far as the train was concerned.

Next, large candles protected by glass cases and having reflectors behind them were used with better results. Big lamps that burned whale oil were extensively used in the 1840's and 1850's. Later, kerosene took the place of whale oil.

Gas lights came next, the gas being supplied from a storage tank carried on the engine. The first patent for an electric headlight was taken out in 1881, and by 1884 the first really successful light of this kind was used on the Pennsylvania Railroad.

HESSIAN FLY   This insect, very destructive to wheat, received its name because it appeared first on Long Island in 1779 near where the British general Lord Howe had encamped three years before with a large number of Hessian soldiers in his army. It was thought the Hessians had brought the pest into this country in the straw they

used for bedding. So the insect received the name *Hessian
fly*.

Nearly thirty thousand German troops were hired by
the British Government to serve in this country during
the Revolution. So many of them were from the province
of Hesse that they were all known as Hessians. Some of
them died in service, and many others decided to remain
here. But about eighteen thousand returned. Not long

after they reached home, this same insect made its appearance in Germany. People there at once associated it
with the returned Hessian soldiers. And they promptly
gave it a German name, *Hessenfliege*, that is, "Hessian
fly," thinking the Hessian soldiers had brought it back
from America in the straw they used for bedding!

HICKORY   The colonists at Jamestown had not
been there long before they noticed that the Indians were
fond of something that looked like mush with milk in it.
That part of Virginia abounded with trees that bore

nuts which the Indians prized highly. They gathered them in great quantities and kept them for use throughout the winter. They prepared them for eating by pounding them in a mortar, breaking up the shells and the kernels together. Then they poured water on this mixture and let it stand for a time until the broken shells became thoroughly soaked and sank to the bottom.

The oily, milky-looking liquor on top of the mixture was called by the Indians *pawcohiccora*. They ate it with bread and also used it in their simple cooking. It looked so much like milk that when the white settlers amazed the Indians by obtaining a somewhat similar-looking liquid from cows, the natives at once called it *pawcohiccora* too.

Apparently, the colonists took this Indian food name, and throwing away the first of it, changed the last part into *hickory* which they used, not for the food, but for the tree which supplied the nuts in the first place.

The tree was of far more use to the settlers than its nuts. Its wood is strong and tough and thus suitable for handles of tools and for making wagons. The heavy mauls the pioneers used in splitting rails to fence their clearings were made of young hickory saplings. Abraham Lincoln was no doubt quite familiar with hickory mauls, for this valuable tree in some of its varieties is found all over the eastern half of the United States.

HOBOMOK SKIPPER   There is a large group of butterflies called "skippers," because of their quick, darting flight. Students of these butterflies, in thinking up new names, have made use of Indian terms, and have coined such expressions as *Indian skipper, Dakota skipper, Pawnee skipper, Pocahontas skipper.*

This last name needs no explanation because everybody knows who Pocahontas was, how she helped the Jamestown colonists, and finally married one of them. But this name was not the first given to this particular butterfly. In 1841 a student of skipper butterflies named this one *Hobomok skipper* and explained the name as referring to "one of our celebrated Indian chiefs."

Hobomok was an Indian warrior who played a part in the Plymouth colony much like that of Pocahontas in the Jamestown settlement. He was a lifelong friend of the colonists and often warned them of plots against them by hostile Indians. Unlike Pocahontas, however, he never married one of the colonists.

His services were so much appreciated that his name lived on among the Plymouth colonists and their descendants. In 1824 a novel was published with this Indian as its hero. In the story, his kindness to the colonists was explained as the result of his devoted love for beautiful Mary Conant, a daughter of one of the colonists.

Mary already had a sweetheart among the young men of the colony, but he was lost at sea—at least, everybody thought he had been lost. So poor Mary married Hobomok, who adored her. But one fine day Mary's first lover at last came home. Hobomok was so noble that, according to the story, he at once gave up all claims to Mary. He restored her to her first love and went away into the far western wilderness to live among his own people.

HOECAKE   Some words are very deceiving, and *hoecake* may be one of them. It looks simple; it seems to be nothing more than the putting together of *hoe* and *cake*. But doubts arise when the matter is studied.

Indians in Rhode Island, and no doubt elsewhere, parched corn and pounded it in a mortar into a coarse meal. They kept this meal in bags made of skins. When they wished to use it, they took out a small quantity, moistened it, and regarded it as sufficient for a meal in itself. The settlers imitated the Indians and were greatly surprised at how nourishing this food was.

From the Indians the colonists learned that the name of this product was something which sounded like *nokehick*. The settlers could not pronounce the Indian term very well, so they called it *nocake*, a word which appears in print at least as early as 1634. After a time the settlers thought of baking this coarse meal into a small cake, which they called *nocake*.

By 1745 *hoecake* began to show up in American writings, and *nocake* declined in popularity. Is *hoecake* a changed form of *nocake?* Nobody has yet found out, but at least two things suggest that it may be. *Nocake* sounds a little like nonsense. To call a small cake of bread a *nocake* is almost a denial that it exists! Yet the explanation that the cakes were named *hoecakes* because they were baked on hoes seems questionable. It is not good for a hoe to bake bread on it, and if the practice is continued, the tool is ruined. Were hoes so plentiful and cheap on the frontier that they could be spoiled in this manner? It hardly seems likely.

HOGNOSED SNAKE   If a creature is found over a wide area, its chances for getting several names are increased. One of the many harmless snakes in this country is a small one found from Massachusetts to central Florida and as far west as central Texas, and in Kansas and eastern Montana.

Two things about this snake account for nearly all the names that have been given it. It has a nose that is slightly turned up. Because of this it is known as *hognose, hog snake,* and *hognosed snake,* this last being its most popular name.

This snake is also one of the best actors in the animal world. When it is alarmed, it puts on quite a show. It spreads the ribs just behind its head in such a way as to form a small "hood" similar to that of the deadly cobra of India. Then it begins giving out short loud hisses, apparently hoping that if its appearance does not frighten away danger, this blowing and hissing will.

These bluffing antics have given rise to many names, such as *blower, blowing adder, blowing snake, blowing viper, blow snake, hissing snake, puff adder, spread head, spreading adder, spreading viper.*

If everything else fails, this little actor pretends to die a terrible death. It writhes about as if suffering horribly, lashing its tail as though in mortal pain, snapping desperately at its own body as though driven quite out of its mind by its dreadful suffering. Finally, it flops over on its back, with its tongue hanging out, and "plays" as if it is quite dead.

HOLLYWOOD   There are thirteen varieties of American holly found chiefly in the Southern states but extending also along the Atlantic coast as far north as Massachusetts. In Alabama, Arkansas, Florida, Georgia, Maryland, Mississippi, and North Carolina, where holly is a native growth, there are places named *Hollywood*. The name has been carried into other states, such as Maine, Minnesota, and California where the holly is not a native growth.

As might be expected, after Hollywood in California became so famous, many stories began to be told about how it received its name. Although there is no real holly native to California, there is found in that state a large shrub or small tree called *California holly* because it bears an abundance of red berries that suggest those of holly and are used at Christmas as ornaments. So it has been thought the presence of this tree suggested the name Hollywood.

Another story is that Mr. and Mrs. H. H. Wilcox, who in 1887 laid out the city, were very pious people and named their town *Holywood*, which in time became *Hollywood*. But those who have studied the matter most think the California Hollywood has a name transferred there from some other place.

HONK   When autumn comes, the large Canadian geese leave their home in Canada and some of the northern states and fly far to the south to spend the winter where it is warmer. They fly in large V-shaped groups, and from time to time they utter a cry which sounds something like *k'honk, k'honk, k'honk*.

Indians in Virginia and other eastern states were well acquainted with these geese and had noticed that when they flew south, giving their well-known cry, winter was not far off. These Indians called the big birds *cohonks* from the cry they made, and they used the same word to mean winter.

The cry of the geese impressed white settlers too, but they used *honk* for the call note of the big birds. Such a word is said to be echoic or imitative. From its habit of making this cry, the Canada goose is sometimes called a *honker*.

More than a century ago, *honk* was used as a verb as well as a noun, and the geese were said to *honk* as they flew south. By the time automobiles came into use, *honk*, both as a noun and a verb, was ready to be used in speaking about the noise made by the horn of the new machine.

The honk of an automobile horn, however, does not much resemble that of a wild goose.

HOOP SNAKE   Early settlers in this country told many strange stories of fearful creatures that lived in the endless forest. The vivid imaginations of those who lived in lonely cabins far ahead of the advancing tide of white settlement added greatly to these stories of strange, deadly creatures said to be found in the dark recesses of the wilderness.

Many tales sprang up among the frontiersmen about the creature named the *hoop snake,* and it was described in detail. It resembled a black snake, but was thicker and shorter, and of a dark brown color. It did not bite, but carried a sharp horn or stinger in the end of its tail, and with this it struck both man and beast with sudden and fatal effects.

When this snake pursued an enemy, it took its tail in its mouth and in the form of a hoop rolled along at such speed that even a fast runner could not escape. The only thing for one to do when chased by a hoop snake was to keep his wits about him and try to jump through the hoop as it flashed past him. Such an exploit called for the nimbleness of a trained acrobat, but when it was done, it so confused the snake that it resumed its ordinary form and went skittering away through the leaves and grass just as any other snake does.

Pioneers enjoyed telling such stories as this around their comfortable firesides with the forest all about them, and with their children listening in wide-eyed wonder at the marvelous exploits of this fearsome imaginary snake.

This wonderful hoop snake had another name, *horn snake,* because of the fearful stinger it was said to have in the end of its tail. This sting was so dreadful that anyone or anything struck by it died at once.

If a man chased by this snake jumped behind a tree

quickly enough, the angry snake would sometimes plunge his stinger into the tree, which would immediately begin to wither. In a few hours its leaves would fall, and in one day the entire tree died.

Tales about this snake grew with the telling, and wonderful stories of marvelous experiences settlers had had with the creature were soon going the rounds. One of the best stories is that of a fat Dutchman who was hoeing

in his field one day when he suddenly saw one of these horn snakes rolling hoop-fashion straight at him.

The poor Dutchman was so frightened that he could not move. In an effort to protect himself, he held the handle of his hoe upright between him and the on-rolling snake. By great good luck the snake stuck its poisonous stinger into the hoe handle and the farmer escaped.

But the hoe handle at once began to swell and soon became so large the farmer could not reach around it. In addition, it became black and blue. The Dutchman watched it carefully for a week, and noticed that the swelling slowly went away. But the metal of the hoe had been so damaged that it was an entire year before it was the fine well-tempered tool it had been before the horn snake had struck its handle.

Both *hoop snake* and *horn snake,* which came into use as names for this wonderful imaginary snake, have been kept in the language; but the snake or snakes to which they are now applied are quite harmless.

HUMMINGBIRD   One American bird received its name from the earliest colonists because of the low, humming sound of its wings, which vibrate far too rapidly for the eye to follow. The bird of this kind that occurs in the eastern half of the United States is the *ruby-throated hummingbird.*

This is certainly one of the most beautiful and remarkable birds in the world, and also one of the smallest. The rubythroat is three and a half inches long and weighs about the same as one cent. The male, with his bronze-green upper parts and brilliant red throat, flashes through the air like a precious jewel in flight.

He often zips along at a great speed, but is able to stop in mid-air and sup the nectar from a tempting flower. He flies backward with ease, and sometimes darts backward and forward as though swinging on an invisible trapeze. He does not hesitate to take off from southern Florida for Yucatan, some five hundred miles away across the Gulf of Mexico.

The Indians were well acquainted with these dainty little creatures and sometimes pressed and dried them to wear in their ears like earrings. The Dutch in New York soon became aware of these beautiful tiny birds, too, and tried in vain to keep them alive as pets. They sometimes preserved them between paper and dried them in the sun and sent them as presents to their friends. This practice has, of course, long ago ceased.

HYDRANT   Had it not been for attacks of yellow fever in such cities as New York, Philadelphia, and Charleston, *hydrant* might never have come into the English language.

In seeking the cause of the fever, the officials in Philadelphia thought perhaps the water used there might be the source of it. At that time people in Philadelphia used water from pumps and wells. But about 1800 a reservoir was constructed and water secured from the Schuylkill River. Underground wooden pipes carried the water to all parts of the city. At convenient places along the streets, there were discharge pipes where people could obtain the water they needed. Someone who knew a little Greek called such a fixture a *hydrant,* since *hydōr* is the Greek word meaning "water."

The first hydrants were not satisfactory, however, so they were soon replaced by a simple form of pump, at which water might be had by householders and by fire companies as well. But these did not entirely suit the needs of the situation either, so about 1803 they were set aside, and regular iron fireplugs were used in their place.

Although the device for which *hydrant* was coined soon passed out of use, and the street fixture that took its place was also quickly discarded, the word *hydrant* proved so popular that it has remained in the language ever since. As a result we now have two names for the same object, *hydrant* and *fireplug,* the first of which was coined here and the second borrowed from England.

INDIAN CORN On the November day in 1492 when Columbus landed on the island of Cuba, he sent some of his men into the interior to look around and see what they could find. When they returned they brought with them a plant which they said produced a grain from which the natives made bread.

Columbus did not know much about botany, but he looked closely at this strange plant and decided it was some kind of grain-producing grass such as the Spanish called *panizo.* So in jotting down his daily record of his famous voyage Columbus referred to the new plant as *panizo*, though the natives had a name for it which sounded as if it should be spelled *m-a-i-z*.

Interest in the strange grain and its New World name quickly spread far and wide in Europe. In England the plant was known as early as 1555 if not before. It was usually called *maize*, the native name having become more popular than *panizo*. Those in England who saw the new plant and the seeds it produced thought it was some kind of wheat, so they often called it *Guinea wheat*, *great wheat*, or *Turkey wheat*.

When the first English settlers reached the coast of Virginia in 1607, they had probably heard about this plant. As they worked with the Indians, learning how to plant the seeds four in a hill so that no seed touched another, and how to fertilize the hills with fish, and finally how to harvest and prepare the crop for food, they no doubt asked their Indian friends what they called the plant. And probably the Virginia Indians told them it was called *poketawes* or *hokotawes*, a name difficult to pronounce.

So the newcomers avoided having to learn a new name by taking two words they already knew and calling the plant *Indian corn*. For a time they also sometimes referred to it as *Indian wheat*, but as they became better acquainted with the plant they were less impressed by its resemblance to wheat, so they dropped it as a name.

Indian corn was soon cut down to *corn*, except in those cases where the full form is needed to make it clear that maize is being referred to, and not "corn" in its British sense of wheat, barley, rye, oats, and the like.

INDIAN SUMMER   This expression is one of the best known weather terms added to the English language in this country. Nobody has ever found out positively why it arose. One story is that the colonists were deceived by the first early frosts into thinking winter was at hand, but the Indians told them another summer was still in store for them. Then when the first chilly weather moderated and the sun came out bright and warm and a hazy stillness prevailed over the fields and woods, the settlers, remembering what the Indians had told them, called this delightful period *Indian summer*.

The Indians had stories which they told to explain the occurrence of this late autumn period of delightful weather. According to one of their legends a great Indian god, Nanahbozhoo, occupied his throne at the North Pole, from which place he overlooked the whole earth and the deeds of all his people. This god always fell asleep when winter set in, but before doing so he filled his great pipe and smoked for days and days. The smoke arising from his pipe produced the beautiful Indian-summer weather and accounted for the haziness or smokiness that often prevails at this season.

Another Indian legend attributed this period of mild hazy weather to the lover Shawondasee, a god dwelling far to the south "in the never-ending Summer," whose life had but one shadow, a secret sorrow, because of "a tall and slender maiden/All alone upon a prairie." Longfellow in *The Song of Hiawatha* has given beautiful expression to this old legend about Indian summer:

> Shawondasee, fat and lazy,
> Had his dwelling far to southward,
> In the drowsy, dreamy sunshine,
> In the never-ending Summer.
> He it was who sent the wood-birds,
> Sent the robin, the Opechee,
> Sent the blue-bird, the Owaissa,
> Sent the Shawshaw, sent the swallow,
> Sent the wild-goose, Wawa, northward,
> Sent the melons and tobacco,
> And the grapes in purple clusters.
> From his pipe the smoke ascending
> Filled the sky with haze and vapor,
> Filled the air with dreamy softness,
> Gave a twinkle to the water,
> Touched the rugged hills with smoothness,
> Brought the tender Indian Summer
> To the melancholy north-land,
> In the dreary Moon of Snow-shoes.

IO MOTH   This name for a handsome moth found all over the eastern United States is likely to puzzle anyone. What in the world does Io (pronounced "eye o,") mean?

In Greek-Roman mythology, Io was the daughter of a river god and the granddaughter of Oceanus, god of the sea. She was so beautiful that Jupiter fell madly in love with her. His wife, Juno, suspected her husband had a sweetheart, and by keeping close watch on him discovered his secret.

One day when Jupiter and Io were strolling by a beautiful river, Juno came upon them so suddenly that Jupiter barely had time to change Io into a beautiful heifer. But Juno knew what had happened, and sweetly asked her husband to make her a present of the heifer. Jupiter, greatly embarrassed, had to do so.

Juno pretended to be delighted with the beautiful creature and appointed Argus, who had a hundred eyes, to keep close watch over the cow day and night. Poor Io! She longed to tell her father of her sad fate, but her only voice now was a stupid bellow. Finally she wrote her name with her hoof in the sand where she knew her father, the river god, would find it. And he did see her signature, but he was helpless to do anything for her.

Jupiter grieved so much for his lost sweetheart that he sent Mercury to slay Argus and set Io free. Mercury with great skill and cunning succeeded in his task, and Io became once more her lovely self. Mercury took the eyes of the slain Argus and scattered them as ornaments on the tail of Juno's peacock where they may still be seen to this day.

And two of them may be seen in the keeping of the Io moth, which has one on each of its hind wings.

ITASCA   For a long time explorers had been trying to find the source of the Mississippi River when in July, 1832, Henry R. Schoolcraft succeeded. With a party of sixteen, including an Indian guide and a minister interested in missionary work, he reached the lake in northern Minnesota which Ozawindib ("Yellow Head,") his guide, said was the source of the Mississippi.

Before he reached the lake, Schoolcraft had asked the minister for a Latin or Greek term meaning "true source." The minister's Latin was not quite equal to this request, but he wrote down *"veritas caput,"* two nouns meaning "truth" and "head." Schoolcraft as he glided along in his canoe studied these two words. He decided to take the last four letters of the first word and the first two letters of the second and combine them into *Itasca.*

It is interesting to speculate on what might have happened if the missionary had written in correct Latin the expression for which he was groping when he wrote *"veritas caput."* If he had written *"verum caput,"* what might Schoolcraft have done? *Erumca* might have appealed to him, and now be a name as well known as *Itasca.*

JAYWALKER   Before automobiles became common, everybody crossed streets where and when they pleased and nobody thought anything about it. The slow horse-and-buggy traffic was easy to avoid.

But early in this century the situation changed. Automobiles made traffic dangerous even to those on foot. At that time the slang word *jay*, meaning a "stupid, silly person; a simpleton," was popular; so by 1917, and perhaps earlier, *jaywalker* and *jaywalk* came into use with reference to one who is so stupid as to cross streets in an unsafe manner.

JINX   In slang use, a person or thing that brings bad luck is said to be a *jinx*. The word itself cannot be said to have originated in this country, for it is merely a respelling of the much older English word, *jynx*, but the meaning we give the term is of American origin.

The same word existed in ancient Greece as the name of the wryneck, a bird related to the woodpecker, that made a cry somewhat like the name the Greeks gave it. The wizards and witches of Greece used to bind this bird to a wheel which they turned, believing it drew men's hearts with it and so charmed them into obedience. Such a procedure was often used to recover an unfaithful lover.

The present slang use of *jinx* has about it a touch of the wizardry which the Greeks associated with their *iynx*, the source of English *jynx*, more than two thousand years ago.

JOHN HANCOCK   Many American expressions
are derived from the names of people. *Baldwin apple,*
Bartlett pear, Chippendale chair, Ferris wheel, Pullman,
and *Yale lock* are good examples, but *John Hancock* is
perhaps the best known. The man of this name was the
wealthiest New Englander who helped the patriots in the
Revolution. He lost much of his wealth during the war,
but when the struggle was over he was by no means poor.

Hancock enjoyed many honors, but perhaps not as many
as he would have liked, for he was anxious to be famous.
He was president of the Continental Congress, nine times
governor of Massachusetts, and a signer of the Declaration
of Independence. But if he had done no more than occupy
these offices, he might today be as little known as many
of those who in their time have held high offices and were
later forgotten. Merely by writing his name so plainly that
it could be easily read he secured a place in the dictionary.

The story is told that when President Hancock sat down
to sign the Declaration of Independence he remarked to
those about him that he would make his signature so large
that John Bull could read it without his glasses. His signature on the Declaration is 4⅞ inches long, but on a letter
he wrote the same year it is only 3¾ inches.

A person's signature is now sometimes called a *John
Hancock* in colloquial language.

JOHNNY APPLESEED   John Chapman was
one of the oddest characters ever seen on the American
frontier. He was born in 1774 in Leominster, in central
Massachusetts, and died in 1845 at Fort Wayne, Indiana.

When he was still a boy he became very interested in
apple trees. Apples were greatly prized everywhere, and
especially on the frontier. Every settler had as large an
orchard as he could manage, and used apples in many
different ways. Young Chapman thought of planting apple
seeds over the frontier wilderness so young trees would
be ready for the settlers when they arrived.

With great leather bags filled with apple seeds which
he secured at cider mills, he was soon a familiar figure in
frontier regions that are now Ohio and Indiana. Early in his
career he received the nickname *Johnny Appleseed.*

He aroused attention wherever he appeared. He was
usually barefoot and tattered. He sometimes slept in some
settler's cabin, but always on the floor. Often he spent the
night in the woods under a tree, or if the weather was
stormy or cold, in a hollow log if he could find one.

He tried never to injure any living thing, not even a
mosquito or fly or rattlesnake. Once when he was traveling
with an Indian friend, a rattlesnake bit him on the hand,
and the Indian promptly killed the snake. But Johnny
chided him for treating so cruelly one of God's lovely creatures. The Indians regarded him as such a peculiar fellow
that they never molested him, even during wars with the
settlers.

Stories told by and about Johnny Appleseed are widespread. Books and plays have been written about him, and many poems and jingles have had him as their subject.

JOHNNYCAKE   From early times Americans have enjoyed a form of bread usually made of corn meal with milk or water, and sometimes eggs, and baked on a griddle. Students of words have never been able to agree on the origin of *johnnycake,* the name that has long been used for this bread.

Some dictionaries explain it as having been at first *Shawnee-cake,* so called because Shawnee Indians made bread of this kind. Others derive *johnnycake* from *journey cake,* such bread being often taken along by those going on long journeys. Perhaps the following explanation is the best one.

Country people in England and Scotland used to be fond of bread made of oatmeal or coarse wheat flour in the form of a small cake baked on the hearth before the fire. Some of them called it *jannock,* but others in different parts of the country pronounced this word differently. They called it *johnnick,* or *johnnick bread,* and they spoke of "cakes" of such bread.

When some of these people came to this country they made bread in just the same way by using the meal of Indian corn. And they called it by several names—*jonakin, jonikin, johnny bread, johnnycake, journey cake.* Of these terms *johnnycake* proved to be the most popular.

JUKE BOX   The origin of *juke* has been often discussed and many efforts made to explain it. One explanation derives it from an Old English word *jook*, or *jouk*, which is said to have meant "to hop or skip about like a bird."

The best explanation that can be given is that *juke* comes from an African word meaning "to lead a disorderly life; to misconduct oneself." *Juke-houses* and *juke-joints*, places of low amusement, have long been known in some parts of the South. These resorts were such disreputable places that more respectable people had them closed, so they are no longer common.

Music boxes were popularly used in these places, and from their being often found in *juke-joints* and *juke-houses* any automatic record player played by coins in slots came to be called a *juke box*.

KATYDID   One of the most common American insects is a large, long-legged green creature somewhat resembling a locust or grasshopper. The male has a rough, filelike structure at the base of its front wings. When he rubs the two wings together he produces a noise which, with a little help from one's imagination, sounds very much like *katy-did, katy-did,* or *katy-didn't, katy-didn't.*

On fine nights in summer and in autumn the males enjoy sitting up in green trees and sounding over and over the note which gives them their name. It is easy for listeners to think those in one tree are saying *katy-did, katy-*

did, and those in an adjoining one are insisting *katy-didn't,
katy-didn't.*

This insect has had poetry written about it. Oliver
Wendell Holmes (1809-94) wrote of it:

> I love to hear thine earnest voice,
>   Wherever thou art hid,
>   Thou testy little dogmatist,
>   Thou pretty Katydid!

But much earlier Philip Freneau (1752-1832), the Poet
of the Revolution, had already honored the insect with a
poem. Here are some of his lines:

> Tell me, what did Caty do?
>   Did she mean to trouble you?
> Why was Caty not forbid
>   To trouble little Caty-did?

> Why continue to complain?
>   Caty tells me she again
> Will not give you plague or pain.

KINDERHOOK   This is one of the oldest and
most interesting place names in this country. It is especially interesting because it helps us to understand how
O.K. (see p. 154) arose.

Kinderhook is the English form of a Dutch name,
Kinder-hoek, which means "Children's point, angle, or
corner." As early as 1616 the Dutch gave this name to a
place on the east side of the Hudson River not far from

Albany. Why they named this spot as they did is not positively known.

One guess is that Henry Hudson named it because when he sailed up the river in the *Half Moon* many Indian children assembled on the bluff there to see his ship go by. Another story is that in very early times a Swedish settler lived at the place and had so many children that Dutch traders thought "Children's Corner" would be a good name for it.

At the time of its first settlement, Kinderhook was the name of a large district of over forty thousand acres bordering on the river. In 1823 this area was divided, and the part of it down by the river was named *Stuyvesant* in honor of a famous Dutch governor.

For a long time after the division, however, people called this section along the river *Old Kinderhook*. It was here that Martin Van Buren, once president of the United States, was born. When some of his friends in New York

City formed a political club in his honor in the spring of
1840, they named their organization *Old Kinderhook Club,*
in allusion to his birthplace. It was their abbreviation for
this club, The Democratic O.K. Club, that launched the
familiar term *O.K.* on its long and very successful career.

KIWANIS   Those who were active in founding a
club to promote good fellowship and civic interests in
Detroit in 1915 desired to secure an attractive Indian
name for their organization. A local historian submitted
some Indian terms among which was *keewanis,* which he
had found in an Indian vocabulary compiled by an early
missionary among the Indians of upper Michigan. The
word meant "to make one's self known," "to impress one's
self."

The spelling of this name was slightly adjusted to make
Kiwanis, and in this form it was adopted by the club as
an official name. It suggests "self-expression," and thus
suits the purpose of Kiwanis clubs.

KLAXON   When automobiles first began to appear on the roads and streets of this country they did not
have horns of any kind. The noise they made and the
moderate speed at which they went made horns unnecessary. But in time it was felt that a warning device was
needed. The first such signal was a hand-operated horn
consisting of a rubber bulb on one end of a brass trumpet.

In 1908 an inventor secured a patent on a horn that was

electrically operated. He coined *Klaxon* as the trade-mark for his new product, and this word has now become popular.

Klaxon is based upon the Greek verb *klazein,* which is related to the Latin word *clangere* from which "clang" comes. The Greek verb means to make a sound of some kind, its precise meaning depending on the source of the

sound. When birds are referred to, it means "to scream," as the eagles and herons do. When dogs are the source of the sound, it means "to bark or bay." If things such as arrows in a quiver are being talked of, *klazein* means "to clash or rattle." If the wind is spoken of, it means "to whistle." If people are referred to, the verb means "to shout or scream."

It would be difficult to coin a word that has in it more of the element of sound than does *Klaxon*.

KODAK   When someone coins a word and explains how he did it, his account has to be accepted as final. But sometimes people find it difficult to believe that the coiner of a word proceeded precisely in the manner he says he did.

In May, 1888, George Eastman, an American industrialist and inventor, made the first of the little cameras which later became so well known. He needed a suitable trademark for his product, and set to work trying to think of one. He later explained that he wanted a short word that could not be misspelled or mispronounced or infringed upon by anyone.

The letter "K" attracted him because it was the first letter of his mother's family name. In thinking over his problem, he thought two "Ks" might be better than one. By associating these letters with others and trying out the resulting expressions he hit upon *Kodak,* which seemed to him just the word he needed. It has been called one of the most successful trade-marks ever coined and has been a part of the language for a long time.

Anyone who studies Mr. Eastman's explanation of how he made this word may wonder if—without his being conscious of it—*Kodiak,* the name of an island in the Gulf of Alaska, or possibly *Kodiak bear,* may have been lurking somewhere in the back of his mind as he worked on the word he sought.

LATCHSTRING, *the latchstring is always out*
Those who lived on the frontier far from villages and towns could not get locks for their doors. They had to use what was at hand, so they made fastenings of wood.

A very common means of keeping a door closed was a wooden latch that could be raised or lowered from the outside by means of a string that passed through a hole in the door. If a settler wished to make sure that no guest entered his house while he was away, he placed this latch in position from the outside by means of the string, and then poked the string through the hole until it fell inside the room.

If he left the latchstring in its usual position, outside the door, anyone could at once get into the house. So the position of the latchstring, inside or outside, indicated something of the hospitable nature of the settler.

In inviting his friends to come to see him, the friendly pioneer would often say, "the latchstring is always out," that is, "my house is at your disposal any time. Come in and make yourself at home, even if I am not there at the moment you arrive." The expression is still used colloquially, and is often seen in print.

LETHEON   Words are mortal, and some of them die when quite young. Many of those coined in this country passed away so soon after their first appearance that dictionaries do not bother to include them. *Letheon* is a word of this kind.

In discussing *anesthesia* (see p. 33), we mentioned that Dr. William T. G. Morton wished to keep secret the nature of the wonderful fluid he was using to render patients temporarily unconscious. For a time the doctors who had seen or heard of his brilliant achievement were completely in the dark as to what the remarkable liquid might be.

During the excitement caused by his wonderful performances, some doctors especially interested in what had been found out met at the home of Dr. Augustus A. Gould, who lived near the site of the present Boston Museum of Fine Arts. At this meeting the question came up of a suitable name for the preparation Morton had discovered. Dr. Gould read off a list of possible names he had jotted down.

One of those he listed was *letheon*. He had invented it, or someone had suggested it to him. No matter who coined it, the name was clearly inspired by *Lethe,* the name of the river of forgetfulness in Hades told about in Greek and Roman mythology. Maybe the common word *oblivion* had suggested a good ending to put on *Lethe*. Dr. Morton at once gave this name his entire approval.

In the letter which Oliver Wendell Holmes wrote to Morton about some possible names, he said the name selected would "be repeated by the tongues of every civilized race of mankind." But despite this grand prediction, *letheon* is not now repeated by the tongues of anybody, and few people indeed ever heard of it. It soon became known that the wonderful, mysterious fluid Morton was using was nothing but ether to which he had added some harmless perfumes, so the fine new word *letheon* was not needed at all.

Dr. Morton's fortunes soon followed that of the word he had approved and used. Others now came forward claiming they had experimented with ether before Morton had, or that they had told him about its effects and so were entitled to a share of the glory and honor of having ushered in painless surgery. The last twenty years of Morton's life were filled with bitter controversy and lawsuits. He died almost insane with worry, and in poverty.

LIGHTNING ROD   In 1744 Benjamin Franklin was thirty-eight years old. That year there came to

Philadelphia where he lived, a Dr. Adam Spencer, of Scotland, who was going about giving lectures on what was then known as "natural philosophy."

Franklin went to hear Dr. Spencer, and was greatly interested in the evening's performance. In the course of his lecture Dr. Spencer performed some clever tricks. He took a small boy and suspended him horizontally from the ceiling by silk threads. Then he rubbed a glass rod vigorously with a silk cloth and presented the rod at the boy's face. At once a bright spark flashed between the end of the rod and the face of the boy. No wonder this trick of the "electrified boy" amazed and delighted the Philadelphians.

The evening's program set Franklin to thinking about electricity, about which very little was then known. One of the first results of his interest and experimenting was his conclusion that lightning and electricity are the same thing. With his famous kite, he proved the correctness of this theory on a hot day in June, 1752, during a thunderstorm.

Franklin's next thought was that it would be possible by means of a long, pointed metal rod to draw off, quietly and harmlessly, the lightning in a cloud. Such a rod could be easily mounted in a way to protect a house or anything else from being struck by lightning. Soon some of the public buildings in Philadelphia were provided with these tall, sharp metal rods.

This invention was the wonder of its time. A name was at once needed for it. Many terms were used. *Conductor, lightning conductor, electric rod, electrical rod,* were among the first to be employed. Some people called the device a *Franklin,* or a *Franklin rod;* and others thought *rod* alone would suffice.

The name that suited everybody best, however, proved to be *lightning rod,* and that name soon became so popular that few people nowadays have ever heard of the other names that were tested out for the new invention.

LISTERINE   There must not be many homes in which there is not kept a supply of an antiseptic known as *Listerine*. This name is based upon that of Sir Joseph Lister, a famous English surgeon and the founder of antiseptic surgery.

By the middle of the nineteenth century it was known that microbes from the air get into wounds and cause them to putrefy. Lister succeeded in perfecting methods to keep microbes away from wounds, and thus made a tremendous contribution to medical progress.

Two physicians in St. Louis, Missouri, soon set about making an antiseptic agent. When they had obtained a product they regarded as highly satisfactory, one of them went to Edinburgh, Scotland, to see Dr. Lister and to secure his permission for the use of his name as the basis of a trade-mark for their product. The eminent surgeon agreed to this proposal, and in 1879 the first Listerine was placed on the market.

LOAFER   Americans are so active and energetic that it is surprising *loafer* originated among them.

The evidence indicates that it is a shortening of *land-loafer*. Dutch *landlooper* or German *Landläufer* had at a much earlier time passed into the English of England, being spelled *landloper,* and meaning "one who runs up and down the land," "vagabond." About the time this borrowing faded out of use in England, *land-looper* (later *land-loafer*) showed up in this country, clearly a fresh borrowing from Dutch or German settlers of the word that had a century earlier resulted in *landloper* in British use.

Land-loafer was felt to be needlessly long, so *loafer* was used alone in the sense of "an idler—one who is too lazy to work." This short form proved so popular here that the verb *loaf* soon appeared, no doubt inspired by the popularity of *loafer* and made from it.

Derivative words such as *loaferdom*, the "kingdom of loafers," *loaferess*, "a female loafer," *loaferish*, and *loaferism* have not continued in use, but the noun *loafing* and the expression *loafing place* are not unusual.

LOG CABIN   It was not until about 1750 that the expression *log cabin* became part of the English language. The first English settlers who came to this country did not build houses of logs because the idea of doing so had never occurred to them. They had never seen such houses in England. But Swedish colonists who settled on Delaware Bay in 1638 knew about log houses and lost no time in building them. Their example was soon followed by English settlers.

No two log cabins were alike. Some were made of small round logs; others were of large logs split in the middle and put up with their round sides exposed to the weather. The spaces between the logs were daubed—or *chinked* as the settlers said—with mud. In summer this *chinking* might be taken out to let in the air and make the cabins cooler.

The roofs of such simple houses were of long boards

split from trees. When nails were not to be had, heavy poles, called *weight poles* by the frontiersmen, were used to hold the roofs in place. Many of the cabins on the frontier did not have any metal at all in them.

Log cabins differed greatly in size. One that was sixteen feet long and twelve feet wide was perhaps average. A porch might be added on one or more sides. Such porches kept the logs from rotting by protecting them from rain and snow. Some cabins did not have any floors. The enclosed earth was pounded until it was hard enough to serve very well for a floor.

The most famous log cabin in the world is the one in which Abraham Lincoln was born on February 12, 1809, in what is now Larue County, Kentucky. It had only a dirt floor, and the chimney, of mud and sticks, was apparently never finished.

LOG CABIN AND HARD CIDER CAMPAIGN   In times of great political excitement, those opposed to a particular candidate sometimes do or say something that makes their opponent's fortune.

In 1840 when William Henry Harrison was running against Martin Van Buren for the presidency of the United States, an enthusiastic supporter of Van Buren suggested that Harrison be given "a barrel of hard cider and a pension of two thousand a year, and, our word for it, he will sit the remainder of his days in a log cabin by the side of a 'sea coal' fire and study moral philosophy."

This sneer became at once the political slogan: "Log

cabin and hard cider," and it resounded from one end of the country to the other. It gave Harrison's friends the opportunity to picture him as a simple man of the frontier —possessing the basic virtues of honesty and heroism, living plainly and studiously—in marked contrast to Van Buren, a New York aristocrat, who was pictured as reveling in luxury and wasting his time with other wealthy sinners of every description.

Harrison won the election easily, though in fact he was a Virginia aristocrat who lived in an exceedingly comfortable home and spent far more time holding office and seeking office than he did in reading moral philosophy— or anything else.

LYNCH   This term arose in connection with the breaking up of the first band of organized criminals in this country.

Before and during the Revolution members of this gang were busy in the frontier regions of both the southern and northern colonies. They had confederates in every colony with whose help they sent booty stolen in the southern frontier settlements to northern ports, and that taken in the north to smugglers off the coast of present-day Georgia and Florida.

The criminals prospered greatly during the troubled times of the Revolution, but on September 22, 1780, some victims of these thieves and murderers on the Virginia frontier organized to put an end to them and their wickedness. They selected as one of their leaders a strong upstanding man of thirty-eight named William Lynch, who had been a soldier in the American army.

This self-appointed law-and-order group succeeded in ridding their frontier settlement of horse thieves and their like, but their disregard of legal procedures set a bad example and made the name of Lynch a part of the English language in an unenviable sense.

After a few years this group of citizens apparently disbanded. Lynch himself served in the Virginia legislature and later moved to the backwoods of South Carolina, where he died on June 15, 1820. A local newspaper in giving an account of his death described him as, "an old Revolutionary soldier, a friend to the widow, and orphan, and a good farmer: he died in possession of Christianity and the good will of all honest people who knew him."

One suspects that the expression "the good will of all honest people who knew him" may have been inspired by the fact that even in 1820, thirty years after the deed, there were those who felt that Mr. Lynch and his friends had disgraced themselves by punishing people without giving them a legal trial.

MALTED MILK   Nearly a century ago James and William Horlick began to manufacture food for babies and invalids. Their product was an extract of wheat and malted barley. Milk was necessary in preparing it for use.

Seeking to improve his product, William Horlick thought of including whole milk with it, and evaporating the entire mixture to dryness. The product he obtained this time was easily transportable, kept well in any climate, and needed only the addition of water to be used.

In 1887 he applied for a patent on this item of food which he described as being "For infants, Invalids, the Aged, and Travelers." He coined the name *Malted Milk* as a trade-mark for this product.

Malted milk is now a well-known soft drink, usually made with ice cream, which is enjoyed by many who do not fall into any of the classes listed above.

MAPLE SIRUP, MAPLE SUGAR   The first settlers along the Atlantic coast learned many things from their Indian neighbors.

They found that the natives made sugar from the sap of maple trees, and of course they quickly followed their example, for at first they had no other source of sugar. Many terms arose from the activities of the frontiersmen in securing their sweets from maples.

Maple water was the sap from the maples; *maple beer* was made by adding a quart of *maple molasses* to four gallons of boiling water. *Maple wine* resulted from adding a suitable amount of yeast to boiling maple water. *Maple vinegar* was easily obtained by allowing maple water to remain for a few hours in the warm sun. *Maple wax* was made by pouring boiling syrup over snow or ice that cooled it quickly. *Maple sirup* is obtained by boiling down the sap of the maple tree, and *maple sugar* results from boiling the maple sirup. These two terms are the best known of those resulting from this kind of sugar-making.

MARCH OF DIMES   Franklin D. Roosevelt
was stricken with infantile paralysis in August, 1921. He
was paralyzed from his waist down, but his magnificent
will was not impaired. Out of his efforts to overcome his
affliction and to help other victims of this crippling disease,
the National Foundation for Infantile Paralysis was organized January 3, 1938. Some of those greatly interested
in working out the details for the organization and in
making plans for financing it held a meeting just before
this, on November 22, 1937. Among those present was
Eddie Cantor, a celebrated comedian.

When the problem of how to secure funds for carrying
on the fight against infantile paralysis came up, Cantor
told of how successful a thirty-second broadcast was that
he had made at the time of a disastrous flood along the
lower Mississippi River. He said he felt sure that all
the national radio programs would devote thirty seconds
to the great cause in which the committee was interested.

The question of a suitable name for this national appeal
came up. Cantor thought of the millions of dimes they
hoped would flow in, and said, "We could call it THE
MARCH OF DIMES." The others present agreed at once
with his suggestion, and this new expression became part
of the language.

MASS MEETING   Sometimes an expression
comes into the language but is not much used until a par-

ticular need for it is felt. This was the case with *anesthesia,* and a similar thing happened with *mass meeting.*

It is known to have been used in 1733 by a New Englander in his diary. It may have been employed before and after this, but evidence of it is not easy to find until the Log Cabin and Hard Cider political campaign of 1840 (see p. 139).

In this battle for the presidency, the newly organized Whig party introduced every political device they could think of to secure votes. Tremendously enthusiastic meetings with thousands present were held, and the term *mass meeting* was used hundreds of times. Parades of all kinds were the order of the day, and such expressions as *torchlight parade, torchlight procession* made their appearance in the language. To attract as much attention as possible, huge leather balls, twenty or thirty feet in diameter, were often rolled in these parades, and the expression *keep the ball rolling* was heard on every hand, and used in campaign songs. *O.K.* (see p. 154) is also associated with this period of intense political excitement.

These terms are still in the language, and when properly understood they bear witness to the unbounded enthusiasm of the Whigs to do just one thing—defeat the Democrats. And as we know, they succeeded.

MAZDA   One of the oldest religions in Persia, now called Iran, is based on the eternal conflict between light and darkness. The god of light, Ahura, is good; and he created everything good and pure and holy. To denote that he possesses wisdom as well as goodness, *mazda,* meaning "wise," was long ago added to his name. He was then called *Ahura Mazda.*

He made all the good stars—486,000 of them—and arranged them like an army to defend heaven. But the god of wickedness made evil stars to oppose their good influence. To this day it is said that some people are born under a lucky star and some under an evil one.

In 1910 the General Electric Company needed a word to denote the fine quality of research and manufacturing service they were using in their business. Electric lamps were among the things they made, and in casting about for a word, this old Persian term *Mazda*—closely associated with and forming part of the name of the god of light—was called to their attention. The company immediately registered it as a trade-mark, and used it so much in connection with their products that it has now become part of the English language. You may be reading this page by the light of a Mazda bulb.

McCOY, *the real McCoy*   This well-known slang phrase has engaged the attention of many investigators. Prominent among those who have been brought forward as the source of the expression is a celebrated boxer named Kid McCoy. But Bill McCoy, a bootlegger, and Tim McCoy, a cowboy, have likewise been suggested as the individual referred to in the phrase.

At the present time, the American expression appears to be a modification of a much older Scottish phrase, *the real*

Mackay, so common that in 1886 Robert Louis Stevenson used it in a letter to one of his friends. Which of the Scottish Mackays gave rise to it is not known.

In Scotland the expression came to be used of whisky, much of which was exported to the United States and Canada. From 1895 to about 1901, Kid McCoy, the American boxer, was quite popular. It has been suggested that perhaps his popularity caused the modification of *the real Mackay* into the one now current in slang use.

MINNEAPOLIS   Charles Hoag was thoughtful as he went to bed on the evening of November 4, 1852. He and the other settlers had for days been wondering about a suitable name for their little frontier village on the Mississippi River at the Falls of Saint Anthony.

Different ones had made suggestions. *Albion, Hennepin, Brooklyn, All Saints, Addiesville,* had been mentioned. Suddenly, before he went to sleep, Hoag had an idea. Why not combine the Indian name *Minnehaha,* meaning

"Laughing Water" (the name of a waterfall near the town), with the Greek *polis,* "city," and have a name *Minnehapolis,* "Laughing Water City," or "City of the Falls"? He ran the name over in his mind; it sounded much better with the *-h-* not pronounced.

He got up early the next morning and told his family about the name he had made. They agreed with him that it was very good indeed. He wrote to the editor of a local newspaper, who was also enthusiastic about the new name.

A meeting of the settlers was held, and this Indian-Greek name met with general approval. Since the *-h-* was not pronounced, someone suggested that it be dropped. This was done, the name thus appearing as it does now.

MOCCASIN   Indian footwear looked more like stockings than shoes. These coverings for the feet came much higher on the leg than ordinary shoes. They were made of tanned skins and sewed with the sinews of animals.

Early settlers found these Indian shoes extremely comfortable and well suited for walking through the woods. They often wore them and took over their Indian name, *moccasin.* The word seems actually to have meant "box" or "case." It is still in everyday use, but the shoes to which the name is now given do not look at all like the shoes the Indians wore.

When white people borrowed a word from the Indians they often made more use of it than the Indians had ever

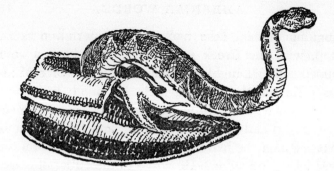

done. They applied *moccasin* to a poisonous snake, the short, stout form and color of which may have suggested the Indian shoe. Most of the early pioneers knew very little about snakes and so gave the name *moccasin* to many snakes, some of which do not much resemble the Indian shoes and are not at all poisonous.

MOCKINGBIRD   Three American birds attracted the special attention of the first settlers in this country. All three have such clearly marked characteristics that they were easy to name. One of them is as red as can be, so he was at once called *redbird*. Another makes such a distinctive humming noise as he flashes about that he was called a *hummingbird* (see p. 115).

The third bird has nothing peculiar about its size or color or general appearance, but its ability to sing and to imitate the notes of other birds is remarkable. *Mockingbird* was the name adopted at once for this fine singer. In the early days of the country many of these birds were captured and carried to England and sold as cage birds.

Stories were told of how these little captives soon became famous as singers in England. It was said that one of them placed in the same cage with a skylark so surpassed this bird in singing that the vanquished bird never dared raise its voice again. And a blackbird placed in the neighborhood of a mockingbird soon drooped and died, so it was said, apparently in despair of equaling this New World singer.

Mockingbirds are friendly creatures and like to live where there are people. Many superstitions have grown up about them. In parts of Kentucky it is said that if a girl puts on a man's hat at night when she hears a mockingbird she will marry that year and have good luck. In some parts of the South it used to be thought that stuttering could be cured by eating the eggs of mockingbirds.

MOOSE   Just as other people have always done, the Indians gave names to animals suggested by something about the creatures that especially impressed them. *Moose* is only slightly altered from the name which the Algonquian Indians gave this huge animal centuries ago.

The Indians noticed that this creature had a peculiar way of feeding. His neck is so short that he cannot graze. When a particularly fine bunch of grass tempts him, he has to get down on his knees to eat it. As a rule, he secures his food by browsing on the tender shoots, twigs, and leaves of trees and shrubs. He sometimes stands on his hind legs and pulls down limbs and branches that grow twelve feet from the ground. Even this is not very high for him, because by running his chin along saplings and branches and so forcing them lower, he is able to strip off leaves that grow twenty feet or more above the ground. One of his favorite ways of obtaining a good meal is to get a slender young aspen tree between his forelegs and "ride" it down so that the brittle stem breaks and he can enjoy its branches at his ease.

No wonder the Indians were greatly impressed by such feeding habits. So they gave this animal a name which in their language meant something like "he strips or eats off." *Moose* is one of the earliest terms borrowed from the Algonquian Indians and may have appeared first in the English spoken in Canada.

MORMON CRICKET   This unusual name for an insect came about from the fact that these cricketlike grasshoppers were the worst enemy imaginable to the early Mormon settlers in Utah.

In the spring of 1848 millions of them fought a terrible battle with the first settlers in the Salt Lake region. The prize they were after was a fine nine-hundred-acre field of wheat that was nearly mature. Wheat meant life itself to the settlers, so fifteen hundred of them—men, women, and children—fought against these creeping, crawling, running destroyers.

The settlers surrounded the field with straw, and when the pests were black upon it, they fired it. They plowed deep trenches around the field and swept the greedy grasshoppers into them and buried them. But millions escaped. The exhausted settlers were losing the battle.

Suddenly the sky was darkened by hundreds of beautiful Franklin's gulls, as large as pigeons. These handsome fellows took sides at once; they gorged themselves on the crickets till they could eat no more. Then they emptied their stomachs and continued the battle.

A faint echo of this remarkable engagement is retained in the well-deserved name *Mormon cricket*. What the grateful settlers did for their beautiful winged helpers in this battle may be seen under *Franklin's gull* (see p. 94).

MOURNING DOVE   As a rule, birds do not appear to be sad, but the mourning dove is different. It has no pretty clothes, but wears a grayish-blue suit, that of the female being even duller in color than that of the male. And its note is not at all cheerful, but gives those who hear it the idea that the bird is mourning about something that is too sad for words.

The sad name, *mourning dove,* is not the only one this bird has. It is also known as *Carolina dove, Carolina pigeon, Carolina turtledove, old-field dove, turtledove,* and *wild dove.*

NATURAL BRIDGE   Mother Nature was at work building bridges in this country long before Columbus was born. The only tools she had to work with were water and sand, but she worked so long and industriously that it is difficult to say how many bridges she built. There are so many that the expression *natural bridge* was added to the language here more than a century ago.

The most famous of these bridges is the one over Cedar Creek about sixteen miles southeast of Lexington, Virginia. There is no telling how long it took the creek to wear away the weaker under-rock, leaving the stronger upper layers to form the bridge. The span of the bridge is ninety feet

Rainbow Bridge

long, and its height above the bed of Cedar Creek is more than two hundred feet. The bridge is from fifty to 150 feet wide. A modern highway crosses it.

Thomas Jefferson once owned the land around this bridge and admired the wonderful structure so much that he built a summer home near-by so he could invite his friends to come and enjoy the sight with him. It is said that George Washington visited the bridge and carved his initials on the rock.

For a long time people thought this bridge was the largest in this country, but in 1909 Paiute Indians guided white men to a much larger one in San Juan County in southern Utah. This one has a span of 278 feet, and the top of it is 309 feet above the now tiny stream responsible for the magnificent spectacle.

The remarkable natural wonder is in a lonely canyon. Indian hunters came upon it and were so impressed by its beautifully colored pink arch that they called it *Rainbow Arch*. The white men the Indians guided over the dangerous way to this unusual spot were so thrilled by the natural curiosity that they asked Congress to preserve the place for future generations to enjoy. Congress acted the following year, and now Rainbow Bridge is a national monument.

NEW YORK   The Dutch were the first Europeans to make a settlement at what is now New York City. As early as 1613 they had a trading post on Manhattan Island, but it was not until 1623 that real colonization began. The Dutch named their colony New Amsterdam.

After a time England and Holland became involved in a war and the English took the city, which they renamed New York in 1664. In England there is a very old city named York. It was the capital of Britain when the Romans occupied the country (A.D. 43-410), so it was natural for Colonel Nicolls, the new English governor, to think New York would be a good name to take the place of New Amsterdam. Then, too, the colonel saw the fine opportunity the situation gave him to pay a compliment to the Duke of York, his friend and patron, who in 1685 became James II, King of England.

O.K.   In the spring of 1840 political excitement was especially high in New York City. The Democrats were more than eager to re-elect Martin Van Buren as president.

In their enthusiasm, some of Van Buren's friends in New York organized a club to further his political interests. On March 23, the secretary of this club placed an announcement in a New York City paper about the next meeting of the organization. This announcement began: "The Democratic O.K. Club are hereby ordered to meet . . ."

The political enemies of the Democrats at once pounced upon this mysterious "O.K. Club," and speculated much on what *O.K.* might stand for. The Democrats, delighted that they had their opponents baffled, for a long time withheld any explanation of the mysterious abbreviation.

Speculation once begun about *O.K.* went on for a little more than a hundred years, during which time all kinds of guesses were made about its origin and meaning. Then in July, 1941, an American professor came upon the solution to the puzzle. And what a simple one it was!

O.K., he found, stood for "Old Kinderhook." The full name of the political club was "The Democratic Old

Kinderhook Club," this name being adopted by way of honoring Van Buren who had been born in Old Kinderhook, New York, not far from Albany (see p. 128).

OPOSSUM   One of the first wild animals the colonists in Virginia became acquainted with was a furred creature about the size of a house cat. They had no name for the animal, so they asked the Indians what they called it. The Indian word was, as usual, a hard one for Europeans to pronounce; but doing the best they could, the settlers made *opossum* of it. This term was soon shortened to *possum*.

The Indians named the opossum because of its color, the meaning of their name being "white animal." This is not an accurate name, for it would suit any animal that is white. In fact, some of the Indians in the Great Lakes region used a form of the same word to mean "a white dog." Besides, not all possums are white. Most of them have a grizzled appearance.

One of the things which impressed the colonists about the possum is that when attacked it seeks safety by pretending to be dead. It puts on an excellent act, falling over limply, shutting its eyes and sticking out its tongue from its half-open mouth. When the enemy passes on, the actor comes to life and runs away.

From this habit of the animal the pioneers coined the expression *to play possum* or *to act possum,* which they used with reference to any activity designed to deceive.

OREGON TRAIL   By 1842, wonderful stories were being told about the fabulous fertility of the Oregon country. Wheat grew taller than a man, oats were eight feet tall with stalks half an inch thick, beets were harvested when three feet around, and turnips when they were five!

No wonder covered wagons filled with pioneers and their families were soon crowding the two-thousand-mile-long Oregon Trail to this remarkable land of promise. The trail began at Independence, Missouri. For a time it skirted the Little Blue River, and then struck straight for the South Platte, which it crossed, and continued on along the south side of the North Platte.

The very names of places along the trail still have an echo of far-off romance about them—Chimney Rock (Nebraska), then Scotts Bluff. Right on the trail went to Fort Laramie (Wyoming), and from there to the North Platte crossing. Then straight west past Independence Rock, a granite boulder on the north bank of the Sweetwater River in central Wyoming, to South Pass, where it got through the Wind River Range. From there the old road led to Soda Springs (Idaho) and the valley of the

Snake River, which it followed till it reached the Columbia River. Then came the last stage of the journey, the
long trek along the Columbia to Fort Vancouver, the
present Vancouver, Washington.

The old route is a historic memory now, but from 1842
to 1860 it was the busiest road in this country.

OSCAR   Every year the members of the Academy
of Motion Picture Arts and Sciences select those who have
during the preceding twelve months made outstanding
contributions to the motion picture industry.

Those honored in this way receive gold-plated statuettes,
thirteen inches high and weighing six pounds, called
Oscars. It is said that Emil Jannings in 1927 received the
first of these awards for the part he played in "The Way
of All Flesh." The following year annual awards were
begun, but the present name for them did not come into
use for another three years.

The story is that on the first day of her employment in
1931, Mrs. Margaret Herrick, later Executive Director of
the Academy, saw one of these little figures and exclaimed,
"Why, it reminds me of my uncle Oscar." Her remark
was overheard and used by a newspaper columnist, and
Oscar in this new sense was soon well known all over the
country.

According to the account, Mrs. Herrick did not have an
uncle Oscar, but she did have a second cousin of that
name. She said later that the similarity between him and
the statuette was purely whimsical on her part.

OUTBOARD MOTOR   The story is told that
on a hot August day, Ole Evinrude, of Milwaukee, and
some friends, among them Ole's future wife, Bess, went
on a picnic to an island near Milwaukee.

During the day Bess expressed a desire for some ice
cream, and Ole, anxious to please her, hopped into a boat
and rowed the long distance necessary to get it. By the
time he got back, the ice cream was entirely melted, and
he was too, almost.

But the episode set him to thinking about a portable
motor which could be attached to a boat when it was
needed. This idea was by no means original with him.
Motor boats had been made for some time. Such a boat,
built by the Steinway Company, famous for its pianos, had
been used in the rescue of six men from Lake Michigan in
plain sight of many visitors to the first World's Fair in
Chicago on September 4, 1893.

Ole Evinrude and his wife, however, succeeded in making the first commercially successful portable motor for
small boats. Different names were at first used for such
motors. An early inventor called his a *boat-propelling device*. *Outboard porto motor* was also used. But as early as
1909 *outboard motor* made its appearance in the language
and was ready for use as the name of the little forty-six-
pound, one and one-half horsepower motor developed by
the Evinrudes.

PAN, *to pan out* When a thing turns out to be profitable, we often say *it panned out well*. When the reverse is the case and something that looked promising proves to be a disappointment or a failure, we say *it has not panned out well*.

This colloquial way of speaking originated among gold miners, who used a pan or gold pan, a bowllike receptacle, for washing out soil that contained small particles of gold.

A miner found gold by putting a suitable amount of promising soil in his gold pan, adding water to it, and washing it thoroughly. Then he carefully poured off the water and earth, and if he was lucky, he might find small particles of gold clinging to the pan.

If there were enough of these to justify his doing so, he went to work with a will and panned out as much as he could. If, however, there were no gold particles or too few to bother with, he went on to another locality to try his luck there.

In the one case the soil had *panned out* well and in the other it had not. From this use of the phrase it has been extended to apply to any kind of undertaking.

PANHANDLE   More than a hundred years ago somebody, noticing that part of the State of Virginia extended up between Ohio and Pennsylvania somewhat like the handle of a pan, called that part of the state the *Panhandle*.

Later, during the Civil War, this area was organized as a separate state named West Virginia. About thirty thousand men from the new state joined the Union forces during the war, and perhaps ten thousand joined the Southern armies. In this way, *Panhandle* was carried far and wide, and resulted in West Virginia's having the nickname *Panhandle State*.

Other states also have *panhandles*. A part of Idaho extends up between Washington and Montana, and this region has been referred to by that name. But the region of this kind that has become the best known is the part of northern Texas between New Mexico and Oklahoma.

The Texas Panhandle is larger than any of the others and is rich in history. In the early days of cattle raising, there were large ranches in this region, and many an adventurous young man left one of the Eastern states to become a cowboy in the far-famed Texas Panhandle.

PAPER WASP   The first paper was made in China, about two thousand years ago. But the Chinese were not really the first papermakers. That honor goes to a widespread and well-known insect less than an inch long that has the habit of chewing dead wood into a pulp and making of it a strong, coarse, paperlike material suitable for the insects' use in building nests. These papermakers are not confined to the United States, but it was in this country they first obtained the name of *paper wasps*.

Some of these wasps like to hang their nests by a very strong stem under the eaves of barns and in other places where the colony is not likely to be disturbed. Others like to build a round- or oval-shaped nest as large as a football. This nest they hang up securely in a tree in the woods. Sometimes ten thousand wasps live in one of these large nests.

The big, handsome tree-dwellers are called *bald-faced hornets* or *white-faced hornets*, because there is a conspicuous white spot on their "faces," that is, the front of their heads. Because of their severe stings they are to be strictly let alone as they go about their business, which is often that of catching houseflies.

Another species of paper wasps are called *yellow jackets* because of their color. They live underground in nests not entirely unlike those of the first class mentioned above. They are hard fighters too, and their sting is far from pleasant.

PASSENGER PIGEON   Early explorers in the United States found pigeons in unbelievably large numbers. One of the things the settlers noticed about them

was that they went from one place to another at particular seasons. At that time *passenger* was used for a bird of
this kind. So the early pioneers called this bird a *passenger
pigeon*, though *migratory pigeon, pigeon of passage, blue-
headed pigeon*, and *wild pigeon* were also used.

The story of these beautiful birds is a sad one. At one
time the largest flocks were numbered in the billions.
Their nesting places were sometimes several miles in
breadth and forty or fifty miles long. Some trees in these
areas would have a hundred nests in them, and others
were broken down entirely by the weight of the birds.
Pioneers sometimes saw flocks passing overhead which
they estimated to be at least a mile wide and 240 miles
long.

For many years after white men came, the number of
these birds did not appear to diminish, but as the country
became more and more populous, and as thousands of
people continued to destroy the birds without regard to
their survival, they began to disappear.

The last one in the whole world died at the Cincinnati
Zoological Park in 1914. We unconsciously refer to this
remarkable bird when we use the expression *stool pigeon*
(see p. 206).

PATHFINDER   The great American novelist,
James Fenimore Cooper, probably never knew it, but he
added a word to the English language. In 1840 his novel
entitled *The Pathfinder*, or *The Inland Sea*, appeared.

In this book, the leading character in all of Cooper's

Leather-Stocking Tales, Natty Bumppo, had the name "Pathfinder," because of his skill in finding his way through the trackless wilderness. The name of the novel got into print a short time before the book itself appeared. It was used in the autumn of 1839 in a notice saying: "Cooper has written a new novel entitled the *Path-finder, or our Inland Seas!"*

All dictionaries now have the word *pathfinder,* but because of lack of space none of them explain that it was at first the name of a character in a novel.

PAUL BUNYAN   Paul Bunyan is the most famous legendary character in the literature of this country. He is the mythical king of all the lumberjacks. Many remarkable stories have been told of him.

When he was born, so the myth says, he was not different from any other baby. But he grew much faster than any ordinary child. When he was six months old his mother began giving him all the maple sirup he wanted, so by the time he was four years old he weighed eighty pounds.

When he was old enough to begin school, he weighed three hundred pounds and thought nothing of walking thirty miles every day to school. He soon got as far as the fifth grade. But he was growing so fast that he had a very hard time getting in at the schoolhouse door. He decided he would have to give up school, though he was only twelve years old. That afternoon, when school was out, Paul picked up his teacher, gave her a big hug and kiss, and told her he could not come back because he was too big for school. She knew he was right, but she liked him very much and hated to see him leave.

By this time he was already nine feet tall, so he went to a logging camp and got a job helping the cook. Later he became a lumberjack. His appetite, which was always good, increased greatly as he worked among the big timber in the clear, cold air. He often ate as many as forty flapjacks for breakfast, each one fried on a special griddle nine feet across. When he was full-grown, he wore a number 39 shirt, and it took seventy yards of cloth to make him a pair of overalls. The sheets on his bed were twenty-five feet long, and even then his feet stuck out from under them.

He was so strong that he could take a huge scythe made specially for him with a blade sixty-two feet long and mow down huge trees. He had an enormous blue ox, named Babe, and easily hauled the trees he had cut to the mill. The road he hauled them over was crooked, so one day he hitched Babe to one end of it and pulled the road out nice and straight.

The other lumberjacks all loved him and would do anything he asked them. He taught them to tell the truth always. This is why all lumberjacks are now so truthful.

PEABODY BIRD   The peabody bird is a pretty little fellow. He is easily the handsomest of the sparrows and when it comes to singing he surpasses them all. His gay song has caused many people to try to express it in words. One of the results is "Ah! Poor Canada, Canada, Canada." Another is "Old Sam Peabody, Peabody, Peabody," and from this interpretation of what he is saying comes one of his common names, *peabody bird*.

This name has had an unfortunate career in dictionaries. As early as 1890 it appeared in the large unabridged Webster's dictionary, a new edition of which came out that year. The explanation given of the name was the correct one, that it comes from the song of the bird. But within a few years another large dictionary came out, and in this one the name of the bird was explained as being derived from that of Peabody Glen in the White Mountains of New Hampshire. Unfortunately, editors of later dictionaries, instead of following the leadership of the 1890 Webster's, took up the Peabody Glen explanation of the bird's name.

Another name for this handsome little songster is *peverly bird*. The story is that Mr. Peverly, a New England farmer, was walking over his farm one fine spring morning and wondering if he should put in his wheat. As he pondered this important question a bird spoke up out of the nearby woods and said, "Sow wheat, Peverly, Peverly, Peverly!"

That settled the matter. Mr. Peverly went ahead with his sowing, and in the autumn an exceptionally abundant harvest was gathered. And ever since this little feathered oracle is often called the *peverly bird*.

PEACE DOLLAR   In November, 1921, President Harding signed a peace treaty which formally ended
World War I between the United States and Germany.
The Treasury Department regarded it as a fitting time to
issue a coin that would commemorate this happy occasion,
so in December, 1921, the Peace Dollar was minted, and
on the following January 3, placed in circulation.

Seldom has a coin excited so much interest and criticism.
Anthony de Francisci was the artist who designed the coin,
but for his guidance he had eight designs other artists had
submitted to the Treasury. The Liberty head on the coin
was a composite one resulting from the efforts by Francisci
to take advantage, as far as possible, of those that had
been submitted.

But this head was immediately criticized. Miss Liberty
appeared to some of the critics to have her mouth open.
Others thought there was nothing about the head to suggest a "Miss," but that it rather resembled that of a ten-
year-old boy. Still others called the coin a *flapper dollar*,
"flapper" being just then popular in slang use for a frivo-
lous teen-age girl.

The main objection to the coin, however, was the lack
of anything about it that emphasized peace except the
word at the bottom of the dated side of the coin. One
critic felt that a dove should have been used in the place
of the usual eagle on the reverse side.

This dollar was issued from 1921 to 1928, and in 1934
and 1935. Since the last date no silver dollars of any kind

have been minted, but if there should be another issue, the design of the Peace Dollar would be the one used.

PEANUT   The idea that nuts grow on trees is so well established that many people are surprised to learn that peanuts grow underground. The low branching plant which produces them has small flowers borne on stems which enter the soil and there produce fruit.

The peanut is now grown in all tropical countries and has many names. In this country it has two names that came from the Congo region in Africa. One of these African names is *goober,* which is often used in the Southern States. The African word from which *goober* comes really means "kidney." When the Congo natives first saw the seed of the plant, and noticed how two of them usually lie close together in the same pod, they thought their word for kidney would be a good one for the nut.

But other natives of the Congo region gave the seed an entirely different name, and this, expressed in English, is *pinder.* Both *goober* and *pinder* as they are used in the South refer usually to the nutlike seed, rather than to the plant which produces them.

The nut is so well known that many names have been given it. *Carolina groundnut, earthnut, goober pea, grass-nut, ground pea,* have all been used in different parts of this country. But *peanut* is the best-established name.

It has been so popular that many expressions, such as *peanut bar, peanut brittle, peanut butter, peanut candy,* have been made with it. Peanuts are so common and cheap that *peanut politics* is sometimes used as a slang term for political activities inspired by mean, unworthy motives. On the same level of usage, we also sometimes say of a thing that it is "Not worth peanuts," or we simply use the word alone as the exclamation, "Peanuts!"

PHILADELPHIA LAWYER, *as smart as a Philadelphia lawyer*   No one has been able to find why Philadelphia lawyers have been regarded from early times as being much smarter than other people.

It is possible that one of the most famous trials in the history of this country gave rise to the expression. Early in the eighteenth century, William S. Cosby arrived in New York as the royal governor of that province. Unfortunately he was a tyrant, and knew nothing about such freedom-loving people as he found in New York.

He was very anxious to make a fortune as quickly as he could, and ruled the province without consideration for the laws or the rights of the people. Among those who opposed his tyrannical measures was John Peter Zenger, a thirty-six-year-old settler from Germany. To aid in the fight against the governor, Zenger began a newspaper in which he gave prominence to essays praising liberty and observance of law. He also published anonymous verses ridiculing the governor.

The aristocratic Cosby arrested Zenger for libel and imprisoned him for nine months in the cellar of the City Hall. He was not allowed to see his wife, but managed to communicate with her through a hole in the door of his prison.

She continued the paper so skillfully that opposition to the governor and his ways increased.

As the trial approached, Zenger and his friends could not secure the services of any New York lawyer because the governor's influence prevented them from appearing. But they were fortunate in getting a noted old Philadelphia lawyer, Andrew Hamilton, who managed the defense so well that Zenger was declared innocent of libel and the haughty governor was sternly warned of the wickedness of his ways.

Enthusiasm over the triumph of liberty and law was very great. Forty leading citizens of New York honored Hamilton at a dinner in the celebrated Black Horse Tavern on what is now Williams Street. He left New York by boat for Perth Amboy, New Jersey, where a stage was waiting to take him to his home in Philadelphia. Upon his arrival at Perth Amboy, he was saluted by all the guns of the ships in the harbor.

The fame of this trial, and praise for the celebrated Philadelphia lawyer who upheld the freedom of the press to print the truth without fear or favor may have given rise to the expression "as smart as a Philadelphia lawyer." Like many other expressions, this one has inspired many guesses about its origin. One of the most popular of these is that in colonial times lawyers trained at Philadelphia had fine reputations. The popularity abroad of Benjamin Franklin, who came from Philadelphia, might have contributed something to the popularity of "Philadelphia lawyer."

PINOCHLE   Words sometimes become con-
fused with others that resemble them and the results are
often interesting.

Pinochle is the result of this kind of confusion. The story
begins with the French word *bésigue,* the name for a card
game quite like pinochle. The origin of this word has not
been found out, but for our purposes it does not matter.
In Switzerland, where French is much used, *bésigue* was
understood by many of those who spoke French as being
bésicles, the French word for "spectacles," or "glasses."

Those who thought the French card game was *bésicles*
understood this name as alluding to the fact that the game
made use of a deck of cards which had two cards of
each kind, just as spectacles have two lenses. So they felt
free to substitute for *bésicles* another French word,
binocle, meaning "opera glasses" or "binoculars."

German is also widely used in Switzerland, and some of
those who spoke it borrowed *binocle,* and in their language
spelled it *Binokel,* or *Binoggel.* When this German word
was brought to this country by those who enjoyed the card
game in question, Americans borrowed it into English in
the form *penuchle, penuckle, pinocle,* and *pinochle,* the
spelling now most often used.

POCAHONTAS   Indians thought of names in a
way that appears strange to people in modern times. They
felt that a person's name was such an intimate part of

him that it should be guarded with great care. Anyone knowing it, they thought, had an advantage over him, and might do him great harm. So the natives kept their real names to themselves.

One of the earliest Indian chiefs the settlers at Jamestown came into contact with appears in history by the name of *Powhatan*. But this was not his real name. His residence at the falls of the James River, located at what is now Richmond, Virginia, was named *Powhatan*, but his real name was *Wahunsonacock*.

He was the father of the most famous Indian girl ever born in this country. When she was small her parents, noticing that she was of an unusually playful disposition, named her *Matoaka*, a name derived from a verb meaning "to play." When white people settled at Jamestown the parents did not want them to find out what her real name was. Captain John Smith said the Indians called her *Pocahontas* "because that the savages did think that, did we know her real name, we should have the power of casting an evil eye upon her." It was under this harmless, pretended name that she became famous.

PODUNK   Any small insignificant place is likely to be called by this name. But there are two places that actually have this name. One of them is in Massachusetts and the other in Connecticut.

Very little is known about the Podunk Indians from whom this place name comes. It is said that in 1631 a chief of this tribe visited the colonists in Massachusetts and invited them to come and see the fertile Connecticut Valley where the Podunks lived. These Indians were not numerous, and they appear to have lost their tribal identity before the year 1700. The meaning of their name is not known.

How *Podunk* came to be used for "any small, inconsequential place" is not easy to make out. But as early as 1877 it was mentioned in a dictionary and defined as, "A term applied to an imaginary place in burlesque writing or speaking."

POINSETTIA   In 1828, Joel R. Poinsett, the United States Minister to Mexico, found there an unusual tropical shrub or herb which is native to Mexico and Central America. It has a rather inconspicuous flower, but the large showy leaves are of beautiful colors, being bright red in some plants.

Because Mr. Poinsett had the good fortune to discover this remarkably beautiful plant, his name, written in the Latin manner *Poinsettia,* was chosen as its genus name. As is often the case with genus names, this one in time came to be used as the common name of any plant belonging to this genus. It is written *poinsettia,* a form which still further disguises the fact that it was originally a personal name.

The poinsettias most often seen in this country are pot plants, whose large, red flowerlike leaves make them very popular ornamental plants at Christmastime.

POLYPHEMUS MOTH   This moth is a giant among its kind, having a wingspread of nearly five and a half inches. On each hind wing it has a large eyelike spot. The size of this moth, and the single eye-spot on each hind wing suggested a suitable name for it.

In Greek mythology Polyphemus was a famous one-eyed giant. The best story about him is the one which tells of how wickedly he treated Ulysses and his companions, and how he suffered for it. On their return from the long war against Troy, Ulysses and some of his men came upon a large cave on an island they were exploring. They were looking about in it when in came the resident of the cave, the giant Polyphemus, driving his flock of sheep before him. Ulysses very humbly identified his friends and himself to the giant and asked Polyphemus for kind treatment.

The giant had already closed the entrance to the cave with a huge rock, so the unfortunate Greeks could not get out. Instead of politely opening his huge rock-door and letting them go on their way, the cruel creature grabbed up two of the Greeks and ate them for supper. The next morning before driving his flock out to pasture he ate two more. He closed the entrance to the cave when he left, thinking he would eat all the Greeks at his leisure.

But Ulysses was the most cunning of all the heroes who fought at Troy. He and his men spent the day in the cave sharpening one end of a great log the giant had brought in with the intention of making a walking stick out of it. That night, for his supper, the giant gorged himself on some more of the Greeks and drank a great quantity of delicious wine Ulysses had given him.

After the stuffed Polyphemus had fallen asleep, Ulysses and his men heated the sharpened end of the great billet of wood in the fire and then plunged it into the single eye of the wicked giant. The monster roared and shouted till the very island echoed with his lamentations.

Ulysses and his men outwitted the giant again the following morning and got safely away.

PONY EXPRESS   A century ago mail was carried across the Great Plains by riders mounted on swift ponies. This system of communication was known as the *pony express*. The most famous of these systems was the one in operation in 1860 and 1861 between St. Joseph, Missouri, and Sacramento, California, which are about fifteen hundred miles apart.

One hundred and ninety stations were built on this long way. Some were as close together as ten miles, but others were as much as twenty, depending upon the nature of the country. Nearly five hundred of the strongest and toughest horses in all the West were stationed along this road. About eighty riders, young men and boys not weighing more than about 135 pounds, were hired.

Each rider covered from forty to over one hundred miles, changing horses at every station. Sometimes, however, the next rider would be unable to take his turn, so the same rider would have to continue. William F. Cody, or Buffalo Bill as he is best known, though only a boy of

fifteen, was one of these riders. He once rode 322 miles in about twenty-two hours. This record was never surpassed.

Mark Twain made a trip over the old stage road which was used by the express riders. He wrote about how exciting it was for those on the stagecoach to see the pony express go by. As soon as the driver of the stage saw the rider in the distance he called out: "Here he comes!" And Twain says:

> Every neck is stretched further, and every eye strained wider. Away across the endless dead level of the prairie a black speck appears against the sky, and it is plain that it moves. Well, I should think so! In a second or two it becomes a horse and rider, rising and falling, rising and falling—sweeping toward us nearer and nearer—growing more and more distinct, more and more sharply defined—nearer and still nearer, and the flutter of the hoofs comes faintly to the ear—another instant a whoop and a hurrah from our upper deck, a wave of the rider's hand, but no reply, and the man and horse burst past our excited faces, and go winging away like a belated fragment of a storm!

This pony express system lasted for sixteen months, and then lightning itself took its place. The electric telegraph connected St. Joseph and Sacramento.

POPCORN   Names coined in this country often seem to suit the objects to which they are applied especially well.

Indians were acquainted with different varieties of corn, and they made at least a little use of a kind whose grains explode when they are heated. Nothing is positively known about the use of such corn by the New England and the Virginia Indians, but it is said that they were acquainted with it, and that they parched it and mixed maple sirup with it to improve its taste.

Indians in the Southwest and Mexico certainly knew about this corn. An early writer says that the native girls who served in the temple of the Aztec god of war painted their cheeks, adorned their arms with richly colored feathers, and "placed over their heads, like orange blossoms, garlands of parched maize." These garlands are believed to have been made of grains of corn that had been exploded by heat.

The small hard grains of this corn contain a little moist starch. When they are exposed to dry heat, the soft starchy part suddenly explodes so violently that the entire grain is turned inside out with a little pop somewhat like the noise of a tiny pistol. So as soon as they became acquainted with corn of this kind, frontiersmen called it *popcorn*. A more suitable name could hardly have been found.

POTATO CHIP   Usually when a new term comes into the language, nobody makes a record of its first appearance or jots down the circumstances under which it was first used. By the time people become interested in its origin, it is often difficult or impossible to find out just when or how the expression arose, and stories spring up to explain the circumstances under which it came into existence.

This is what happened in the case of *potato chip*. It is not known positively who used it first, but it seems likely that both the term and the thing it denotes appeared first in Saratoga, New York. One indication that this was the place of origin is that such chips are sometimes called *Saratoga chips*, or *Saratoga potatoes*.

The most popular story of how potatoes in this form became famous is this one: In 1853 in a well-known restaurant in Saratoga, a patron who was very particular about his food sent his potatoes back to the kitchen, saying that they were too thick and not thoroughly done. The chef, George Crum, partially of Indian descent, was very proud of his reputation as a cook, so when he received the order returned in this way, he vowed to prepare potatoes thin enough for this fastidious customer. He sliced some as thin as paper, put them in ice water, and then dried them in a towel before dropping them into a kettle of boiling fat. Much to his surprise, they came out nicely browned, curled at the edge, and quite crisp. He salted them and sent them to the dissatisfied customer.

When the customer sampled them he was more than delighted, and so were all who had a taste of them. From that time on, the popularity of potato chips was assured.

POTLATCH   Europeans found that the natives in this country had some peculiar ideas about gifts. When an Indian gave a present he expected one in return. When he found he was not going to get it, he took his present back. Under these circumstances *Indian gift* and *Indian giver* were added to the language.

The Indians living along the coast from northwest Washington to southern Alaska have a strange ceremonial feast called a *potlatch* at which time the host gives away all he has to his guests. *Potlatch* has nothing to do with a pot or a latch, but is based upon a native term, *patshatl,* which means "a gift" or "giving."

For years a man and his wife may work diligently, collecting property of all kinds, especially choice furs and fine blankets. When they have become wealthy, they announce a potlatch and send invitations far and wide. Often theirs is a house-building potlatch. Each guest upon arriving is assigned a task. They cut down trees, hew planks, make carvings, prepare food. In a remarkably short time they complete the house and assemble for feasting, singing, and dancing.

When the fun is at its height a hush falls on the assembly, and as everyone watches, a curtain at one end of the main room is drawn aside, and there stand the host and hostess in their most gorgeous finery beside a treasure of costly blankets and furs and food. The guests applaud just as if they were in a theater.

Then the giving of presents begins. No one is missed. Each one receives a present suited to his or her rank until the man and his wife are stripped of the last thing of value they possess except the house in which they live.

But they have acquired honor and reverence that will make them forever afterward people of importance. And best of all, they can now sit back and take things easy as long as they live, for every guest, by accepting a present, pledged himself to give in due time one of equal or greater value in return.

PRAIRIE SCHOONER   Before railroads were built in the West, the United States had military posts along the North Platte River, and in many other places of the "far West" of that time.

The soldiers at these outposts had to be fed, and supplies had to be kept there for use as payments to the Indians for their lands. Thousands of tons of flour, bacon, sugar, coffee, tobacco, and other supplies were transported to these distant posts by huge covered wagons carrying about three and a half tons and often having attached behind them a trailer with an additional ton or two. Many of them were drawn by plodding oxen.

Seen at a distance across the plains these huge vehicles with their white canvas tops looked somewhat like ves-

sels at sea, and were often referred to as *prairie schooners*.
Many of them were modified Conestoga wagons (see
p. 71) which received a new name because of their use
on the prairies.

PULLMAN   When railroads began to be built
in this country, there was at once need for a name for the
vehicles which ran on the tracks to carry passengers and
freight. Americans met this need by taking the old words
car and *coach* and giving them extra work to do by serving
in this new way.

It was not long before someone made a car on which
passengers could lie down and sleep as they continued
their journey through the night. For this new type of vehicle the name *sleeping car* was at once used. The first such
car ran on what is now the Pennsylvania Railroad between
Harrisburg and Chambersburg during the winter of 1836-
1837.

In 1864 George Mortimer Pullman (1831-1897), a young
Chicago contractor, decided to disregard costs and build
a really fine sleeping car. Up to that time the most that
had ever been spent for a passenger car was five thousand
dollars. Pullman built his first sleeping car at Chicago
and named it the "Pioneer." It cost more than twenty
thousand dollars, a great sum in that day.

It was placed in service in the spring of 1865. Such cars
soon became so well-known that the older term, *sleeping
car*, is now seldom heard. *Pullman car* or more often, *Pullman*, has taken its place.

QUONSET HUT   This term may pass entirely
out of the language, but it has been widely used in the
sense of a prefabricated temporary shelter of special steel
construction, insulated inside with wood fiber, and shaped
like a huge half cylinder.

Such structures were widely used during World War II
and served as homes for millions of American soldiers. It
is said they were designed by Frederick Wierk. They received their name because the first ones were used at the
naval air station at Quonset Point, Rhode Island.

Quonset is an Indian term, but its meaning has thus far
not been made out. It is said to have been shortened from
the much longer *Seconiquonset,* but the significance of
this fuller form is not now known.

RADIO   Many people now living are older than
radio. This term became part of the English language
about sixty years ago.

Early in this century, when the brilliant Italian physicist
Marconi showed the world the way to wireless communi-
cations, inventors and interested students everywhere
began putting up sending stations. No license was needed.
Everyone could do as he pleased in this wonderful field.

Many new expressions came into use, such as *radio-
telegraph, radiotelegraphy, radiotelegram, radioteleph-
ony.* Although *wireless* had at first been widely used
here, as it still is in England, it was not long until these
longer expressions led to the adoption in this country of

the much shorter term *radio* for all kinds of wireless communication.

Other countries also made use of this short, easy word.
It is now a part of such languages as German, Italian,
Spanish, and Swedish. Even in England it has made gains
on the older term *wireless*, and is often used.

Radio goes back to the Latin word *radius*, which meant
a "beam" or "ray" as well as a "spoke of a wheel."

RATTLESNAKE   One of the first American
creatures mentioned in reports sent back to England was
a poisonous snake having a hard, bony structure at the
end of its tail with which it makes a shrill, rattling noise
when it is excited that may be heard twenty yards away.
It was this peculiarity that gave it the name *rattlesnake*
quite early.

Almost as soon as the creature became known, fables
began to grow up about it. In 1674 a writer told of how
this snake was the chief, or captain, of all the other snakes.
He said that in some places such snakes were found on
one side of a river, and if taken across the stream into the
woods on the other side, they died at once.

This author said that the fat of a rattlesnake is excellent
for frozen limbs, bruises, lameness, aches, sprains, and
the like. He also favored his readers with the information
that the heart of such a snake, dried and pulverized and
drunk with wine or beer, was the best remedy against the
bite of the creature.

As time went on, other superstitions were added to

these. The skins of rattlesnakes were made into belts and worn to keep off rheumatism. They were also used as hatbands and sometimes as neckties.

Rattlesnake has entered into many other expressions. In many pioneer households *rattlesnake grease* and *rattlesnake oil* were kept on hand for use in almost any kind of sickness or injury. Those who lived in the forest used such expressions as *rattlesnake fern* and *rattlesnake grass* for plants that in some way suggested these snakes. *Rattlesnake master, rattlesnake root, rattlesnake weed,* were so called because the plants were thought to be beneficial in cases of snakebite.

And rattlesnake has been found useful also as the second part of names for different kinds of rattlesnakes, such as *banded, black, diamondback, prairie rattlesnake.*

ROAD RUNNER   In the southwestern part of the United States there is a long-tailed bird two feet tall with some remarkable peculiarities that have won him many names. He thinks it is fine fun to jump out in the

road and run a race with a horseman or a team or even an automobile. For a short distance he can run as fast as a runner of a school track team, but he soon has to give up on automobiles. From his unusual fondness for racing he is called *road runner, prairie runner,* and *runner bird.*

He is not a town bird. He likes to live out in the dry prairie country among the cactus and mesquite and chaparral. Because of his preference for such places he is also called *chaparral cock* and *prairie cock.* The Spanish in the Southwest call him *paisano,* that is, "countryman," and this name has been borrowed by those who speak English.

He likes to eat snakes, and he pounces upon and kills everyone he comes across, even rattlesnakes. Since he has this habit, he is also called *rattlesnake killer* and *snake killer.* He thinks lizards are choice tidbits, too, and catches everyone he can find. So another name for him is *lizard killer.*

It certainly looks like these are enough names for one bird, but the road runner has at least one more. He looks somewhat like his relative the cuckoo; but he spends most of his time on the ground and is therefore sometimes called a *ground cuckoo.*

ROCKING CHAIR   It hardly seems possible that *rocking chair* could have been first used in the United States. But no early British use of the term has been found, and when such chairs came to the attention of people in England more than a hundred years ago they regarded them as American inventions.

British visitors at that time were interested in rocking chairs, which they considered curious novelties "essential to the comfort of the Americans, whether at sea or on land, in a fashionable drawing room, or in the cabin of a ship." One traveler called them "fine tributes to indolence, invented in Boston, and long since common to all America." A more crabbed visitor indicated that in his opinion nobody but idiots would sit in such things.

It is sometimes said that Benjamin Franklin invented the first rocking chair. A prominent minister once visited him and wrote about some unusual things Franklin had:

> He also showed us his long artificial arm and hand, for taking down and putting books up on high shelves which are out of reach; and his great armed chair, with rockers, and a large fan placed over it, with which he fans himself, keeps off the flies, etc., while he sits reading, with only a small motion of his foot.

Even if Franklin did not invent the rocking chair, he at least had one and had equipped it in an unusual way.

ROW, *to have a hard row to hoe,* etc.   From early times Americans have been well acquainted with rows. Many colloquial expressions have grown out of this acquaintance.

If a person has a difficult time of it, he is handicapped, or if luck seems to be against him, he is said *to have a hard row to hoe.* The allusion here is to a row in a field where the grass and weeds have about choked out the corn or cotton or other crop that has been planted and it is a difficult job to use a hoe to rescue what is to be saved.

If one has *a long row to hoe*, then he has undertaken something it will take a long time to complete. If he plans to finish college and then go to medical school and become a doctor, he has *a long row to hoe*. But if he has plenty of courage and energy and goes ahead without any assistance from others he is said *to hoe his own row*.

When one has done the best he can and is utterly exhausted and worn out without means to go farther in what he has undertaken, then he is *at the end of his row*.

SAND PAINTING   Some of the native Indians in the Southwest make remarkable pictures, chiefly of sand. Used for ceremonial and healing purposes, the art of making them has a long history among the Indians.

The Navaho, who use them for healing, are outstanding among those who make these *sand paintings* as they are usually called, though *dry paintings, sand altars, sand mosaics,* are other names for them. The representations, which are sometimes ten or twelve feet in diameter, are made by the medicine men, who use material colored in the five sacred colors of the Navaho—white, blue, yellow, black, and red. Powdered charcoal supplies the black coloring matter, and crushed flowers help with some of the others.

According to old legends among the Navaho, the gods once lived among them but long ago withdrew into the rainbow, and after that the people began to represent the gods in these paintings and impersonate them in dances to drive away the evil spirits.

The paintings represent Mother Earth, Father Sky, Dawn Boy, the Sun, the Moon, and many other things and creatures which the Indians believe have powers, including Dontso, the fly. The medicine man, having made a suitable picture by trickling the sand and pigments from his hand, begins an appropriate chant, and while he is giving it he touches the pictured powers and then the patient so as to transfer some of their strength to the sick one.

Before sundown each day he releases the magic force in the painting by obliterating it with a plumed wand.

SANTA CLAUS   There is no character better known or better loved by American children than Santa Claus. This "right jolly old elf" who is "dressed all in fur from his head to his foot," has several other names, and all of them were given him in the United States.

The two names by which he is best known, *Santa Claus* and *Saint Nicholas,* are both derived from the Dutch who settled in New York. They associated *Sant Nikolaas* with the practice of giving presents to children and friends. By way of honoring this good saint, the Dutch had a festival on the evening of December 6, the feast day set aside for him, and the giving of gifts was a feature of their merrymaking.

Those who spoke English enjoyed the good time on the eve of Saint Nicholas so much that they brought the saint and the custom of giving gifts into their own celebration of Christmas. And Saint Nicholas became with them, just as among the Dutch, the bringer of gifts and the dispenser of joy.

The Dutch pronounced *Sant Nikolaas* so rapidly that what they said sounded very much like *Sinterklaas.* Those who spoke English imitated the Dutch in this pronunciation and made *Santa Claus* out of the word.

The Germans who settled in Pennsylvania also knew about Saint Nicholas, but their name for him was *Pelznickel,* a term made up of *Pelz,* meaning "fur," and *Nickel,* their spelling of the name Nicholas. This name alluded to his wearing furs when he came on the eve of the day set aside to honor him, bringing gifts for good children and rods for the backs of those who had not been good.

English-speaking settlers borrowed *Pelznickel,* changing it into *Belshnickle* in the process. And they brought over to Christmas the celebration of the feast of the saint. *Belshnickle,* meaning "Santa Claus" and "Christmas," was not widely known out of the Pennsylvania-German area and may now have passed out of use entirely.

Belshnickle had a rough manner that made him more feared than loved. He was terror to evildoers among the children, and his harsh ways and the use of his whip impressed them more than the nuts and sweetmeats he distributed. There soon grew up a feeling that the kindnesses he bestowed should be attributed not to him but to the holy Christ child whose birthday was celebrated at Christmas.

So the custom arose of giving love and honor to the

Christkindl, as the Germans called "the Christ child," at Christmas time. Those who spoke English adopted this German word in the form *Kriss Kringle* and applied it to *Santa Claus,* who brings gifts to children without being too harsh if they have not been good.

Whether he is called *Santa Claus* or *St. Nick* or *Saint Nicholas* or *Belshnickle* or *Kriss Kringle* he is the same short, fat, jolly, long-bearded old man wearing a red suit trimmed with white fur. This way of representing Santa Claus was begun by Thomas Nast, a famous illustrator whose parents brought him to this country from Bavaria when he was a boy.

He was employed to illustrate some Christmas poems, and in deciding on a figure to represent Santa Claus he remembered that when he was a boy in southern Germany every Christmas there came round a fur-clad, bearded old man distributing cakes and toys to children.

The picture Nast drew of this friend of his childhood at once became so popular that it has been the picture of Santa Claus ever since.

SAVINGS BANK   There are probably very few children who do not have a little bank of some kind in which they save pennies and nickels and dimes.

Such little banks first made their appearance in this country soon after the Civil War. Before that time small coins were not in common circulation; tokens issued by merchants and certificates and stamps for small amounts had been popular instead. As soon as small coins became

common, Americans began to make what were called
savings banks. This term was not a new one, but the
meaning given it here was.

These clever little mechanical banks for children were
of many types. One kind consisted of the head and bust
of a clown. When a coin was placed in the clown's out-
stretched hand, and a lever in the back was pressed, the
clown raised his hand and deposited the coin in his mouth.

Another type represented a dentist pulling a man's
tooth. When a coin was placed in the dentist's pocket and
a button was pushed, the dentist tilted over backward,
pulling his patient and the chair with him, and the coin
fell into a receptacle.

These early banks have become collectors' items, but
the much simpler ones now in use are still called *savings
banks* or *coin banks* or *dime banks.* A *pig bank* or *piggy
bank* is usually in the form of a pig and has to be broken
to get at its contents, but these terms are now commonly
used to mean any small coin bank.

The term *savings bank* is now also used of a banking
establishment which receives savings and pays interest on
them.

SEEING EYE DOG   After World War I nearly
all the countries that took part in it began to train dogs
to guide men who had lost their sight in the war. In January, 1929, Mrs. Dorothy Harrison Eustis founded the
Seeing Eye, Inc., in the United States. The object of this
organization is to secure and train dogs to lead the blind,

and to train applicants in the proper use and handling of the dogs.

The dogs selected for training are chiefly German shepherds, though boxers, Labrador retrievers, and others are also used. Their training begins when they are about fourteen months old, and lasts for about three months. They are taught to obey—and on occasion not to obey— four commands: forward, right, left, halt. If the dog sees that to obey a command would result in danger for the master, he disobeys and tries to find another solution for the problem.

Dogs are thought to be color blind, so they are not taught to watch traffic lights at street crossings, but to watch traffic. Only when it stops will they obey a command to lead their owner forward.

The expression *Seeing Eye dog* is so new that it has not yet found its way into all the dictionaries, but it is in the latest ones. It is a good example of how new things and new activities are continually making it necessary for new words to be brought into the language.

SEQUOIA   Some of the first explorers in California found along the northern coast not far from the ocean a group of the most remarkable trees in the world. They are huge evergreens, their trunks of rough, reddish bark sometimes reaching a diameter of twenty-seven feet. The tallest one that has been measured goes up 364 feet.

A good name for these remarkable trees was not difficult to find. The reddish appearance of the bark and the color of the heartwood of the trees suggested that they be called *redwoods.* So this old word was given a new duty to perform by serving as the name for these magnificent trees.

Some years after these trees had been found, relatives of theirs were discovered further to the east. On the western slopes of the Sierra Nevada Mountains, at elevations of four thousand to eighty-five hundred feet, even larger trees were growing. On the average they are not as tall as the redwoods, though they reach heights of three

hundred feet and more. Measured ten feet from the ground, the largest trees are from twenty-seven to thirty feet in diameter, and one old giant has been found that measures more than one hundred feet around its trunk.

They are the most massive living things on earth. It is not possible to weigh one of them, but it has been estimated that one of the largest would exceed two thousand tons. A name often used for these monarchs of the forest is simply *big trees*, a term that hardly does them justice. Fortunately both they and their near relatives on the coast are generally known as *sequoias*, a more worthy name that came about in an unusual manner.

About 1760 in a Cherokee Indian village in eastern Tennessee a boy named Sequoya was born. When he was perhaps forty years old he turned his attention to perfecting symbols that would enable his people to read and write the Cherokee language. His friends and relatives laughed at him, and when he persisted in his efforts, decided he had lost his mind. But he finally succeeded!

When Sequoya had completed his system, any Cherokee who had studied it a little could read and write his language just as white people do theirs. The Cherokees were the only Indians who had such a fine way to preserve their history and traditions. They now honored Sequoya for his noble work in their behalf.

He died in 1843, and in some way an account of his remarkable life and achievement reached around the world to Hungary. Perhaps Moravian missionaries from that country who worked among the Cherokees carried his story to their homeland. About this time Stephan

Ladislaus Endlicher, a fine Hungarian scholar who was greatly interested in botany, was studying the extremely interesting trees in California which he had heard about.

In a work he published in 1847 Endlicher used *Sequoia* as the genus name for the California redwoods and the big trees farther from the coast. This splendid tribute to a remarkable Indian scholar has been kept. The scientific name of the redwoods is *Sequoia sempervirens,* and that of the big trees is *Sequoia gigantea.*

And *sequoia* is now often used for either of these great California trees, the big trees being sometimes distinguished as *giant sequoias.*

SEWING MACHINE   This expression must have been used many times, both in the United States and in England, before it appeared in print. Because the earliest printed example found so far occurs in this country, and because an American invented the first practical machine that would sew, *sewing machine* is thought to be one of the many terms added to the English language in the United States.

One of the early American inventors who worked on a machine that would sew was Walter Hunt, a New York Quaker. He made a successful machine, but he gave up trying to improve it, turning his inventive talents elsewhere because he did not wish to go on with a machine that he thought would injure the chances of a living for so many poor people who sewed by hand.

An extremely poor man, Elias Howe, Jr., of Boston, could

not afford such consideration for hand-sewers. He made a machine that would sew, but he could not get people to try it, because they felt it was wicked to deprive poor women, many of them widows, of their livelihood. He exhibited it everywhere he could. He took it to a clothing factory in Boston and offered to sew any seam brought to him. For two weeks he demonstrated his invention and then challenged five of the swiftest seamstresses to sew in competition with his machine. His machine won the contest, but his troubles were by no means over.

However, in the late summer of 1846 he secured a patent on his invention, and it was in connection with this patent that the first example known of the expression *sewing machine* appears.

SHENANDOAH   Many American rivers retain Indian names, and this is one of the most beautiful of all those that have been taken into English. At first glance, it would seem to be more difficult to pronounce than it really is. The first syllable is stressed a little, but the main stress is on the *do: Shen-an-dō-ah.*

Scholars have done their best to learn what the name meant in the Indian language from which it comes. They have not been able to find out definitely, nor have they agreed in their guesses. Some think the word it came from meant "spruce river," and that the name referred to the fact that the stream ran through fine forests of spruce trees.

Other scholars have thought a more beautiful interpretation of the name is justified, and that "Daughter of the Stars" or "River of the Stars" might be a more suitable rendering of the thought the Indians had in mind when they named the stream. By exercising a little imagination, those favoring this view feel that perhaps on clear, starry nights the Indians, looking down from their wigwams high up in the Allegheny and Blue Ridge mountains at the beautiful river flowing quietly far beneath them, saw hundreds and thousands of stars mirrored in its clear waters, and therefore gave the stream a name which connected it with the stars of heaven.

It is to be hoped that this pleasant explanation is the correct one.

SKUNK   The New England settlers soon made the acquaintance of a pretty little animal somewhat resembling a house cat. The colonists were not long in learning that they should give it a wide berth because of the use it made of an ill-smelling secretion as a means of defense.

The settlers inquired of the Indians as to the name of this animal, and out of what the natives told them they made *skunk*.

Skunk is one of the most useful of the words borrowed from the Indians. Even in modern times the skunk is hardly a popular animal, and his reputation in pioneer times was such that the custom arose of referring to a contemptible person as a skunk. The word is sometimes still heard in this slang sense.

The word has also been used in many combinations. The wolverine is sometimes called a *skunk bear* because it has musk glands similar to those of the skunk and its shape is somewhat like that of a small bear. In some places a bobolink is called a *skunk blackbird* because in summer the males have black-and-white markings suggestive of those of a skunk. *Skunk fat* and *skunk oil* were valued in pioneer times because they were thought to be helpful in cases of rheumatism. *Skunk farm* and *skunk farmer* are other combinations into which the word has entered.

The word is often used as a verb, too. In slang use, *to skunk* one's opponent in a game is to defeat him utterly, not permitting him to get a single point or score.

SKYSCRAPER   Early in October, 1871, the city of Chicago was almost entirely destroyed by a fire which left nearly half of its citizens homeless.

Rebuilding began at once, for the need was most urgent. Architects were among those who worked day and night to provide homes and offices for people who had lost everything they had. Among these architects and engineers one of the most brilliant was the then thirty-nine-year-old William Le Baron Jenney. Iron had been used in the frames of buildings for more than fifty years. The idea occurred to Jenney that it would be possible to make buildings much higher by having the iron framework support the outside walls as well as the interior structure.

In 1883 he had an opportunity to try his new idea when he received the commission to build the Chicago office of the Home Insurance Company. The building he erected was the wonder of its time. It was the first to employ steel skeleton construction and was ten stories high, much taller than any building ever before erected. It was the first *skyscraper*, a term now so common for a high building that few people realize that to begin with a *skyscraper* was a triangular sail used high on the mast of sailing vessels before steamships came into use.

SLEIGH   The same word in one form or another is often borrowed into a language more than once.

Before the first settlers ever came to Plymouth in Massachusetts, the following words had appeared in the English language: *slead, sled, sledge*. They had been borrowed at different times from some of the Germanic people living along the coast of the Continent across the English Channel from England. They are all essentially the same word and had come from what was approximately the same source.

By the time the New England settlers became well established in their new homes, they made use of the word *slay* in the sense of a "slead" or "sled" or "sledge." Since the earliest evidence for *slay* in this sense comes from New England, one is justified in suspecting that when the Pilgrims were in Holland before coming to this country they had made the acquaintance of the Dutch *slee*, used for a vehicle which traveled on snow and ice. *Slee* was identical with, or closely related to, those words that had already passed into English in the forms mentioned above.

When the Pilgrims reached Plymouth in the dead of winter, there was plenty of snow and ice to remind them of Holland. No doubt in their new homes they found it convenient to use vehicles like those they knew were popular among the Dutch. And they called this new vehicle a *slay*, because this is just the way the Dutch were pronouncing *slee*.

The spelling *slay*, however, did not last long. The popularity of the common verb *slay*, meaning "to kill," may have inspired a new spelling. Anyhow, *sleigh* was soon substituted, and in that form the word is now firmly established in the language.

SMOKEY   During World War II the need for preventing the dreadful waste caused by forest fires was especially urgent. Officials of the Forest Service in the Department of Agriculture enlisted the help of advertising agencies to assist in cautioning everybody to be careful with fire.

Some of those interested felt that a carefully selected symbol might help direct the attention of all who saw it to the urgent need to protect the forests. They decided that the symbol should be a drawing of an animal that lives in the forest and therefore has a life-and-death interest in the prevention of fires. In 1945 they asked Albert Staehle, a cover artist for the *Saturday Evening Post* and an expert in animal art, to do a special poster for use in the campaign then being waged in behalf of the national forests.

Staehle drew the first of the pictures of the little bear, which are now well-known. But he needed a name for the little forest philosopher. Someone happened to think of Smokey Joe Ryan, at the time a famous New York fire chief, and suggested the name *Smokey*, which was at once adopted.

Smokey's name wasn't included in the first drawing of him that appeared, but in 1948 one of the advertisers suggested that it be put on the bear's forest-ranger's hat or on his belt buckle. Now it often appears in both places.

Another one of the co-operating experts thought it would be helpful if a live Smokey could be used in special campaigns whenever possible. So in 1950 a bear cub that had been rescued from a forest fire in New Mexico was named Smokey. He was flown to Washington, D.C., in a special plane and presented to the National Zoo where thousands of children have had the pleasure of seeing him and associating him with the drawings they already know.

SODA FOUNTAIN   About 150 years ago people began to drink soda water. At first this was nothing but water in which a small amount of soda was present, and to which a little flavoring had been added.

The drink was soon improved by forcing a colorless gas into the water and keeping it there under pressure. When the pressure is removed, the water sparkles and foams in an agreeable manner as the gas escapes. More and more flavors were thought of and used as time went on.

Because it was necessary to keep such water under pressure, it was placed in strong cylinders that soon came to be called *fountains*. The entire apparatus used in keeping and dispensing soda water was called a *soda-water fountain* or *soda fountain*. At first such fountains were not altogether safe, for the pressure inside them could cause an explosion. A newspaper reported in July, 1835, that in New York "a soda water fountain, while two of the shopmen were carrying it in the street, exploded with a tremendous report." But great improvements were soon made, both in the fountains themselves and the drinks they dispense.

SPELLING BEE   Spelling has always been a difficult, tedious subject. Teachers from early times have thought up ways of making it as attractive as possible.

One of the earliest methods was that of having two pupils compete to see which one could correctly spell the most words. In the days of log-cabin schools in this country, teachers often asked groups of students to spell against rival groups.

These occasions were welcome entertainment during the long winter months when other means of social recreation were unknown. Settlers and their families came long distances to these gatherings which were known as *spelling schools* or *spelling matches* or most often, *spelling bees*.

These contests became increasingly popular. Spelling books and the Bible were ransacked for hard words. Ambitious pupils made out long lists of those that often brought disaster to contestants. A popular spelling book of the time included such monsters as *caoutchouc, ghoul, litigious, pelisse,* in a back section meant to be used for spelling bees.

One of the most elaborate of these *spelling bees* was held in Philadelphia at the Academy of Music on March 25, 1875, with four thousand present to see and hear eighty competitors spell against each other. Excitement ran high sometimes. One contestant spelled *reseat* for *receipt* and refused to sit down when asked to do so by the master of ceremonies, contending he had spelled the word right; that it was a "double-header" and could be spelled two ways. The matter was put up to the audience. They roared their approval of the *reseat* spelling, and the contestant stayed in.

Finally only six champions remained standing. One by one, five of them went down on the following: *hawser, infinitesimal, distention, testaceous, purview.*

Spelling bees declined in popularity about 1900, but spelling did not get any easier. Within a few decades poor spelling became so common that spelling bees once more became popular. Local champions were pitted against others in public contests. Interest spread, and state champions were selected. Then these state winners engaged in a national contest known as the National Spelling Bee.

In the 1958 contest a fourteen-year-old girl in the eighth grade from McPherson, Kansas, won the national spelling championship by spelling *propylaeum,* and then the finishing word *syllepsis.*

SQUASH   The settlers in New England soon learned that the natives were fond of a kind of pumpkin which they called *askútasquash, askoot-asquash*. This name signified "it is green, raw, or immature," and alludes to the fact that the fruit is eaten when young and tender.

The colonists also enjoyed this vegetable, and borrowed the Indian name for it, but it was a very difficult one to spell or pronounce. Some of the spellings they used for it were *isquouterquash, isquoutersquash, squontersquash, squanter-squash*.

From such spellings it is obvious that it was the first part of the word that gave trouble; the last part was rather easy. So after a time the settlers threw away the troublesome first part of the native name and kept only the easy last part, *squash*.

It is remarkable how many combinations this word entered into. Not only are there such expressions as *squash beetle, squash borer, squash bug;* but there are many more in which squash is the second element, as *acorn squash, crookneck squash, Hubbard squash, summer squash, winter squash*.

STAKES, *to pull up stakes*   When one decides to leave the place where he has been living and make his home elsewhere, he may say that he plans *to pull up stakes*. This is a very old colloquial expression, and it appears to have originated in the United States.

Positive proof is lacking, but it seems to have come into

use from the way land was parceled out to settlers in early times. Apparently the land set aside for the use of a particular settler was marked off by stakes to indicate its boundaries.

When a settler decided to give up the land that had been allotted him and go elsewhere, it may have been customary for him to remove the stakes to his holding and thus clear the land for assignment to some other colonist.

STEAMBOAT   This word came into the English language in this country at least as early as 1785.

The first man to build a steamboat that worked and was used in regular river-passenger traffic was John Fitch. He built several boats, each one showing improvement over the earlier one, but he was never able to interest people in what he was doing, nor could he secure the financial help he needed. Poor John Fitch had much more than his share of failure.

He once went into the potash business, but his partner ran away with all the money needed in the work. He tried to make buttons, but his factory burned. He became a surveyor and secured some work in Kentucky, but Indians captured him and held him a prisoner for a long time.

He had his usual bad luck with boats propelled by steam. No wonder he became greatly discouraged! But he never for a moment doubted that someone else would succeed where he had failed. When he died in 1798, he left a written request that he be buried on the shores of the Ohio River so that he might lie "where the song of the boatmen would enliven the stillness of my resting place, and the music of the steam engine soothe my spirit."

Less than ten years after Fitch died, Robert Fulton made a great success with his steamboat, the *Clermont*, named after the countryseat of Robert R. Livingston, Fulton's wealthy friend and patron. But it was in connection with John Fitch and his much more obscure efforts that the need arose for the word *steamboat*.

STOOL PIGEON   At one time there were millions of passenger pigeons in the United States (see p. 161), but these birds were destroyed so ruthlessly that today not even one is left.

Those who took pigeons often used nets. They would get a large net and set it in such a way that they could close it from a blind or screen behind which they lay in wait. To lure their prey, they tied live pigeons they had previously captured to stools or supports that could be moved up and down with strings from the hunters' places of concealment.

If wild pigeons appeared overhead, they noticed the captive decoys on the stools or stands below. When the flock wheeled and settled where the captives were, the fowlers closed the net and often captured as many as three or four hundred pigeons at one time.

From this practice, it is thought, came the expression *stool pigeon*, which is now used for one who informs on another, or entices or decoys another into evil of some kind.

ST. PETERSBURG   There are two places in
the United States having this name. One is a small town
in Pennsylvania, and the other is a large, fashionable resort city in Florida.

On February 17, 1880, a terrorist blew up the imperial
dining room of the Winter Palace in St. Petersburg (now
called Leningrad), Russia. If this tragedy had never occurred, there would not have been a St. Petersburg,
Florida.

Immediately after the bombing of the dining room, the
Russian Government made life hard for those aristocrats
suspected of having "liberal" views. Although he had
nothing to do with the bombing, a handsome Russian
aristocrat, Piotr Alexewitch Dementief, quietly slipped
away to America.

He modified his name to Peter A. Demens and became
an industrious, enterprising citizen. After a time he secured
an interest in the Orange Belt Railroad in Florida. Among
those engaged in this enterprise he was the most enthusiastic, and it was mainly through his efforts that the road
was pushed south to what he regarded as the best deep-
water port south of Pensacola.

He was anxious to name one of the towns along the railroad after his birthplace, and the terminal hamlet at the
end of the line was his last chance. On September 5, 1887,
months before his associates had thought about a name, he
referred to the place as "St. Petersburgh" in a letter. His

friends made no protest because they felt sure the town would never amount to anything, anyway, and so the name for it would not matter.

How wrong they were and how wise Demens was!

STUMP, *to take the stump,* etc.   In pioneer times the United States might well have been called the "Land of Stumps." In clearing their fields the early settlers could not take time to remove the stumps of the trees they cut down, so a field would be dotted with remains of what had once been trees. Since stumps were so numerous, it is not surprising that many expressions arose involving this word.

Often a stump made a suitable platform for a public speaker, who by using it became a *stump speaker* and delivered a *stump speech.* Political speeches were often made from stumps, so the expression *to take the stump* came to mean to go around making campaign speeches.

Early roads were frequently nothing more than cleared and widened trails through the forest. Stumps left in them were sometimes so high that a wagon trying to pass over them was brought to a sudden, jolting halt by striking them. So *to run against a stump* came to mean to meet with a difficulty of any kind.

In the forest there were often tall stumps where a storm had broken a tree fifteen or twenty feet or more from the ground. When an animal such as a coon or bear sought refuge by going up one of these tall stumps, he was often in great difficulty, for though he had escaped the pursuing dogs he was at the mercy of the hunter who might be following them. He had nowhere to hide and so fell an easy victim to the hunter's rifle. This kind of situation caused the pioneers to speak of one in a difficult or embarrassing position as being *up a stump*.

If one pretends to do something he is not really desirous of accomplishing, he is said to be *whipping* or *beating the devil around a stump*. In this way he tries to gain favor with those who wish him to do a certain thing and with those who hope he does not do so. The devil enjoys this kind of beating, because he can easily dodge behind the stump so that the blows aimed at him really fall on it.

SUSQUEHANNA   Like Shenandoah, this is one of the most beautiful Indian names that has entered the American language. The credit for being the first English-speaking explorer to write the word belongs to Captain John Smith of the Jamestown settlement. He did not use the present spelling but did the best he could to reproduce the Indian word as he heard it.

Smith understood the word as being the name of a tribe of unusually large, noble Indians living on the Susquehanna River. Early explorers had great difficulty talking with the natives, and it is no wonder that many mistakes were made. Even now students are not sure what *Susquehanna* means, though the idea that it means "muddy or roily river" is widely held.

It is said that one student who puzzled over the make-up of the word regarded it as Latin and separated it into its parts as follows: *Sus,* pig; *que,* and; *Hanna,* the name of a girl. This investigator explained the name as meaning "Hannah and her pig."

Whatever the word meant as the Indians used it, we may rest assured that they had no thought of Hannah and her pig in their use of it.

SWEET CORN   There are many varieties of Indian corn. As white settlements spread westward over this country, frontiersmen often found the Indians using corn that differed from that nearer the Atlantic seacoast.

There is a story that a Captain Bagnal of Plymouth, Massachusetts, in 1779 returned home from a military expedition bringing with him some corn which he said he found among some of the natives on the Susquehanna River. He said the Indians called it *papoon corn.* It differed from other corn in being especially sweet. Its Indian name, *papoon,* it was thought, might be related to *papoose,* and might allude to the fact that the Indians gave their children, or "papooses," corn of this kind.

This story may be a myth, just as some scholars think it is. Nobody has yet found convincing evidence that at the time of Columbus' arrival the Indians were growing sweet corn. More may be found out at any time, but so far as is known now Thomas Jefferson was the first to use the expression *sweet corn.*

He kept a record of what he did in his garden. On April 28, 1810, he noted that he had planted some "Sweet or shriveled corn in the N.W. corner" of one of his garden plots. Perhaps this new kind of corn did not do well, for Jefferson did not mention it again.

TAXI, TAXICAB   Early in 1907 Mr. Harry N. Allen of New York, who was escorting a young lady through the city, took a cab from Broadway at Forty-fourth Street to Fifty-eighth Street, about three quarters of a mile. The driver of the horse-drawn vehicle charged him five dollars for the short ride.

Mr. Allen paid this unreasonable price but determined to do something about the cab system in New York. Automobiles were just then coming into use. Many people jokingly called them "smoke-wagons," and predicted they would never amount to much. Despite this attitude, Mr. Allen thought of using automobiles as cabs.

Unable to get in the United States a small reliable, economical car such as was needed, he went to France and found there just what he wanted. He ordered a number of four-cylinder, 16-horsepower cars of a rich shad color, lined with gray.

On Monday night, October 1, 1907, Mr. Allen gave a public demonstration of the comfort and dependability of these new cabs by taking the dinner guests of the Plaza Hotel in New York for a free ride about the city in sixty-five of them. The drivers of the cabs wore uniforms of gray-blue cloth trimmed with black braid. This demonstration was the beginning of the end for horse-drawn cabs.

Mr. Allen coined the word *taxicab*. He made it by taking the French word *taximètre*, which at that time meant a meter that estimates the tax or fare on horse-drawn cabs, and the word *cab,* a short, popular form derived from *cabriolet.* He combined these two terms into *taximeter cab,* which in actual use was soon shortened to *taxicab* and then to *taxi.*

TEDDY BEAR   President Theodore Roosevelt, or "Teddy," as he was familiarly called, greatly enjoyed hunting. In the autumn of 1902 he took a few days off to go bear hunting in Mississippi.

The hunt was a failure, for not a bear did the President kill. On the last day of the hunt, one of his friends brought a frightened bear cub into camp as a joke and told the noted hunter he might shoot it. Mr. Roosevelt took one look at the miserable little creature, and said "Take it away. I draw the line. If I shot that little fellow, I couldn't look my own boys in the face again."

When the President got back to Washington he told his good friend, Clifford K. Berryman, a cartoonist on the *Washington Post,* about the joke his friend had played on him. The cartoonist was so amused by the incident that he drew a cartoon of it showing Mr. Roosevelt refusing to shoot the little bear.

This cartoon swept the country, and soon everyone was talking about the *Teddy bear.* Toy makers at once began to turn out little stuffed bears by the tens of thousands, and *teddy bear,* both the term and the thing it denotes, became well established in American life.

TOBOGGAN   The first French explorers in Canada found that in winter the Indians used a small, crudely made hand-sled or drag. These sleds were used especially by women for bringing home the game the men killed. In its simplest form, the sled was made of the skin of a deer, but often it was made of wood or branches of trees.

The Indians called this contrivance by a name which the French wrote down in various forms, as *tabaganne, tabagone, tobogan.* When those who used English borrowed the word from the French they also had trouble with it, trying such spellings as *tabagane, tabagine, tobagan,* and finally *toboggan.*

During the time the spelling of the word was unsettled, in parts of New England this kind of sled was called a *tom pung,* a term arrived at by trying to make sense out of the original word. This expression looks so much like a proper name that it was sometimes written *Tom Pung.* But in time, the first part of it was thrown away, and *pung* only was left.

So in parts of New England a crude homemade sleigh, usually a big box on runners, is called a *pung.* This term is very unlike *toboggan,* but they go back to the same Indian word. And a pung certainly does not resemble a toboggan.

TOMBIGBEE   The river of this name is one of the two largest in Alabama. From merely looking at the name of the stream one might conclude that it possibly preserves the name of a settler named Mr. Tom Bigbee but such is not the case. The word is unlike any other in the entire country in alluding to a peculiar burial custom among the Choctaw Indians.

These Indians kept the bones of their dead with great care, putting them in crude boxes or coffins made of young willow trees or similar small growth. Willows grew in such abundance along the Tombigbee River that the stream was called in the Choctaw language *Itumbi-bikpi*, meaning "box-maker." The French were the first to write this word down as *Tambeche, Tombecbe;* and out of their versions *Tombigbee* was adopted into English.

TRACTOR   *Tractor* is another of the words that have been coined more than once. It has been coined twice in this country.

Soon after the Revolution, Dr. Elisha Perkins of Norwich, Connecticut, began to treat local inflammations and pains in a novel way. He made two small naillike pieces of metal, one of iron and the other of brass. When a patient was suffering from pain of any kind, the doctor drew these two bars in parallel fashion over the afflicted part for perhaps twenty minutes.

Such an unusual treatment must have surprised his patients. As the doctor went about his work—no doubt explaining learnedly that this treatment was entirely new, as it certainly was!—and made use of electricity by setting up a current between the points of the different metals used, the patient's astonishment must have blotted out all thoughts of his pain, for in nearly every instance those treated were entirely cured or greatly relieved.

The fame of the Norwich doctor spread far and wide. A name was needed for the little pieces of metal he used. The doctor, or someone else, called them *tractors,* a name made from Latin *trahere* meaning "to draw or pull." Also known as *metallic tractors* or *Perkins' tractors,* they were always used in pairs. The doctor patented his wonderful invention and made the tractors himself, selling them for twenty-five dollars a pair.

Other doctors refused to believe at all in this new remedy, and the Connecticut Medical Society expelled Dr. Perkins as a quack. But he had become known abroad, and many thought he had made a great contribution to medical science.

Suddenly the whole delusion collapsed. A doctor in Bath, England, suspected that it was the imaginations of Dr. Perkins' patients that made him famous. The Bath physician found that he could achieve similar results in his practice by using two little painted sticks!

The tractors had no mysterious power at all. As faith in them vanished the names used for them, along with *Perkinism, Perkinist,* passed out of use.

Nearly a hundred years after people had forgotten about Dr. Perkins and his foolish invention, *tractor* came into the English language again.

It was used in Chicago in 1889 by George H. Edwards, an inventor. In July of that year he applied for a patent for what he called "a certain new and useful improvement in tractors." The machine he had invented was a steam engine that propelled itself on an endless belt or track that passed around its wheels. Tractors are now of many types and use gasoline instead of steam.

It is somewhat odd that Edwards used *tractor* as though it was a common word which everyone would understand. No trace has been found of its use in the sense he gave it before he made application for his patent in July, 1889.

TRAVELOGUE   It is always pleasant to come upon a word whose coiner is known. Burton Holmes is credited, and no doubt justly, with having first used *travelogue,* a term which first appeared in print in 1903.

Scholars sometimes express their vexation at words that are made improperly. *Travelogue* was criticized as being "irregularly formed," because the first part of it is from French and the *-logue* part is Greek. It is a pity that those who know so well how perfect words should be produced seldom make any themselves. Despite its "irregularity," *travelogue,* meaning "a lecture, usually with pictures, describing travels," is now well established in the language.

TREE, *to bark up the wrong tree*   Raccoons were once so numerous in some parts of the country that they seriously damaged corn crops. Ripe corn is highly prized by coons, and they will go long distances if necessary to enjoy a good feast of it. And when grandpa and grandma coon and all the brothers and sisters and uncles and aunts and cousins and friends decide to go along, the poor settler who had built himself a log cabin in the wilderness and hoped to raise enough corn on the little patch he had cleared to feed his family could hardly rest, knowing that every night mass meetings of raccoons were being held at his expense. So he often took down his rifle and with his dog to help him he set out to defend what was his.

The raccoon is a very sly fellow. By the time the pioneer arrived at the scene of destruction with such friends and dogs as he might have rounded up to help him, every coon had scampered up a tree and was waiting to see what would happen. The dogs in the attacking party had no trouble picking up the trails of the coons and following them to the trees. There they would set up a barking to announce that this was the tree the rascal had climbed.

But Mr. Raccoon was smart enough to anticipate this, and he often selected a tree to climb that would enable him to use its branches to cross over to another tree. So if luck was with him, he could continue his way in the treetops for a considerable distance from the tree he had originally climbed, leaving the poor dog barking up the wrong tree.

So when one is misdirecting his efforts and missing the goal at which he aims, he is said to be *barking up the wrong tree.*

TUXEDO   Among the Delaware Indians there was a group or subtribe who called themselves *Ptuksit.*

To white people this name sounded like *Took-seat*. Apparently it was made of two words, and meant "round foot." It is thought that the Indians chose this name for their group in secret allusion to a wolf, "he of the round foot." They selected the wolf as the symbol of their group and thought of themselves as the "Wolf tribe" or subtribe.

White people finally spelled the word *Tuxedo* and used it as the name for a small town and lake about forty miles northwest of New York City. The land around this lake was later included in what is known as Tuxedo Park, and a country club was organized there.

About 1890 members of this club began wearing a tailless dinner jacket which soon got the name *Tuxedo coat*. It was not long before *Tuxedo* was used alone for a suit which is worn by men on occasions that are not so formal as to call for a full-dress suit. Later the word was written without a capital, *tuxedo*, and sometimes shortened to *tux*.

One who is wearing a *tuxedo* is sometimes said to be *tuxedoed*.

TYPEWRITER   Inventors had been trying for more than a hundred years to make a satisfactory writing machine when finally in 1868 Christopher Latham Sholes produced one that became more popular than any of the others.

In his application for a patent on his machine, Sholes called it a *typewriter*. So far as has been found, that was the first time this word was ever used. As soon as such machines became common, there was need for other words in connection with them.

At first it was felt that one who operated such a machine should be called a *typer*, and this word got into a dictionary brought out in 1909 with the definition: "A person who uses a typewriter."

It was soon found that women and girls could operate such machines quite well, and for a time they were called *type girls, typewriter girls,* and *typewriters.* Newspaper accounts sometimes mentioned *typewriters,* including information on how much they made per month and how they frequently married their employers.

There were a few people who thought the machine should be called a *typine,* with the accent on the second syllable. This suggestion did not meet with favor, because *typewriter,* the word Sholes had used, satisfied everybody.

As soon as authors began to type their articles, stories, and books some people thought a new word was needed. *Manuscript* comes from two Latin words meaning "hand" and "write" and signifies "hand-written." Those who were unhappy about using this word for typed material invented *typescript,* and this Americanism is widely used.

UNCLE SAM   When a nickname begins to be used in print, an explanation sometimes accompanies it. Such early explanations are valued by students, because they are more likely to be accurate than stories that appear much later.

In a newspaper published in Troy, New York, on September 7, 1813, the following sentence occurs in an account of recent troubles between Government customhouse officers and smugglers: "'Loss upon loss, and no ill luck stirring but what lights upon *UNCLE SAM'S* shoulders,' exclaim the Government editors, in every part of the country."

In a note to this news story the following explanation is given of *Uncle Sam*: "This cant name for our government has got almost as current as 'John Bull.' The letters U.S. on the government wagons, etc., are supposed to have given rise to it."

In 1842 a book appeared in which the story was told that *Uncle Sam* had been inspired by the fact that Samuel Wilson, a well-known citizen of Troy, was called "Uncle Sam" by his friends. During the War of 1812, so the story said, Uncle Sam Wilson had been an inspector of meat sold to the United States Army.

He stamped the barrels of meat he examined with the letters U.S. to denote that they were now the property of the United States. Some of his fellow workmen, knowing he was usually called "Uncle Sam," jokingly accused him of putting his own initials, "U.S.," on the barrels of meat. This joke went the rounds among the soldiers, so the story said, and the nickname *Uncle Sam* became widespread.

With or without any assistance from this joke, the nickname has become the most popular of those that have originated in the United States.

UNITED NATIONS   When the first European
settlers came to this country the Iroquois Indians had an
organization embracing five of their chief tribes. In 1722
the Tuscaroras joined the confederation which then had six
tribes. The settlers usually referred to the Indians of this
organization as the Five Nations or the Six Nations, but
sometimes they called them the *United Nations*. When
frontier days were over and the Indians gone, this term
passed out of use, and was virtually forgotten.

In December, 1941, twenty-six nations agreed to co-
operate in the great war then going on. They needed a
name for their organization. For a time they searched in
vain for a suitable title. President Franklin D. Roosevelt
and Prime Minister Winston Churchill stayed up late on
December 30, but could not think of a suitable term.

The next morning President Roosevelt waked earlier
then usual, and as he lay in bed he ran over in his mind
suggestions that had been made about a name. As he did
so, the expression *United Nations* popped into his mind.
He was well pleased with it. He rose at once to go to
Mr. Churchill who was his guest at the White House.

He found the Prime Minister in his tub, but hailed him
at once with the query: "How about 'United Nations' "?
Mr. Churchill took a final dip, rinsed the soap from his
eyes, and with his face dripping, looked up at his host
and said: "That should do it."

So for the second time *United Nations* became a part of
the language.

VASELINE   Early settlers in western New York
and Pennsylvania often came upon springs and streams
whose waters had an oily film on them. The Seneca Indians
had found this oil useful in treating cuts, burns, scratches,
etc. The settlers collected it and sold it as *Seneca Oil,*
Indian Oil, or *Genesee Oil.* It was a prized household
remedy.

In 1858 a young New England schoolteacher named
George H. Bissell wondered if he could not obtain a richer
grade of oil by boring a well. He employed a friend,
Edwin L. Drake, to drill a well near Titusville, Pennsylvania. The few people then living in the community
thought boring a well to get oil was a foolish thing indeed,
and they called the undertaking "Drake's Folly."

But on August 27, 1859, Drake and his helpers struck
natural petroleum at a depth of about seventy feet, and
Drake's Folly became a "gold mine." News of the find
spread rapidly, and a rush to the oil region immediately
began.

Among those who heard of the exciting discovery was
Robert A. Chesebrough, a twenty-two-year-old Brooklyn
chemist who was having a hard time producing kerosene
from coal. He realized at once that if twenty-five barrels of
rich, natural petroleum could be pumped from a well in a
single day, as he had heard was being done at Titusville,
his little business was ruined. With his last meager savings
he bought a ticket to the scene of the oil boom.

At Titusville he saw the pumps bringing up natural

petroleum. As he watched he saw a workman scraping or cleaning a waxy substance from the pump rods. He learned this was an oily residue called *rod-wax*, and that it was a nuisance in working the pumps. He found also that when the workmen got cut or scratched or bruised or burned they were glad enough to use this rod-wax as a soothing and healing ointment. Chesebrough took some of it home and succeeded in preparing a jellylike product from it.

By testing his preparation on himself he found that it was an excellent remedy and that it could be used either internally or externally. He patented it at once, giving it the trade-mark name *Vaseline*. In making this word, Chesebrough took parts of German *Wasser*, "water," and Greek *elaion*, "olive oil," and a common suffix of Latin origin, *-ine*. He might in this way have arrived at *Waseline*, but he took advantage of the fact that the German *w* has the sound of *v*, and *Vaseline* was the result.

VENUS'S-FLYTRAP   There are thousands of insects that destroy plants, but there are not many plants that destroy insects. The most remarkable one of this type is the Venus's-flytrap, which is native to eastern North and South Carolina. It has small, regular white flowers on a central stalk from four to twelve inches high.

At the end of each of its root-leaves there is a kidney-shaped blade fashioned into a trap. On the flat surface of this open blade there are six very sensitive erect hairs, three on each side of the middle of the leaf-trap. These hairs are really triggers. When an insect lights on the trap

it is bound to touch one of them. At once the trap begins to close, and a sticky juice oozes on the surface of it. This natural flypaper holds the insect until the trap has closed, which it does in about ten seconds.

The pressure exerted by the two halves of the trap is sufficient to crush soft insects. Others are soon suffocated in the sticky fluid the trap produces. Glands in the leaf begin at once to secrete digestive juices. In eight to fourteen days the insect, with the exception of its hard skeleton, is eaten up. The trap then opens, bends over to spit out the indigestible skeleton, and waits for another victim.

Plants always have at least two names, a scientific one and a common one. The remarkable plant just described received both such names in 1770 from John Ellis, an English naturalist. The scientific name he used was *Dionaea muscipula*. The common name coined at the same time is *Venus's-flytrap*.

The scientific name is a learned way of saying "Dione's mousetrap," Dione being one of the names of Aphrodite, the Greek goddess of love. When Ellis coined the common name, he substituted *Venus*, the Roman name for the Greek goddess of love, and with more regard for the plant's powers, he substituted *flytrap* for *mousetrap*.

WAMPUM   Very often when American settlers borrowed a word from the Indians, they threw away parts of it and kept only a little of the full native expression. This happened in the case of *hickory, raccoon,* and *squash*. But certainly in the case of one word, and perhaps others, the colonists took an Indian expression and made two words out of it.

All over this country the natives used a form of money made of shells. The New England colonists became familiar with this currency, called by the Indians *wampumpeak, wampumpeage, wampompeag.*

The colonists did not have much trouble with this expression, and used it in the form *wampumpeag.* But many among them felt the word was too long. Some of them accordingly kept the first part of it and used *wampum* alone. Others thought the last part of the full term would be sufficient and retained the *peag* or *peak* part.

Different Indians used different names for their shell money. The Virginia settlers became familiar with this New World type of money somewhat sooner than those in New England and found that the natives there called it *roanoke*—not the same word, apparently, as the place name *Roanoke.*

When white settlers crossed the Mississippi River, some of them found that the Mohave Indians had a form of shell money which they called *pook.* Like the Indians in the East, the Mohaves drilled these bits of shell and strung them on strings. A string a foot long was sufficient to purchase a horse.

Natives in the northern part of California called their shell money *ali-qua-chick,* a name white people express as *allocochick.* In Oregon and the Northwest generally, the first explorers and settlers found that the natives called their money *hiaqua.* Pioneers took up this name and used it for a time, but it may be obsolete by now.

Of all the names the natives had for their money, *wampum* has surpassed the others in popularity. It has become so well known that perhaps not many people ever heard of the other names for native shell money.

WARRIORS' PATH   The original highway engineers in this country were animals and Indians. They laid out the first trails through the vast forests of the Eastern states and the plains of the far West.

Indians were great traders and hunters and warriors. They often went long distances to surprise their enemies or to trade with their friends. Those in New York sometimes made raids as far west as the Black Hills in South Dakota and Wyoming, bringing prisoners back from that distant region.

Wherever and whenever possible, the Indians used trails already provided by animals. Where there were none of these, they made some of their own. All they needed was a path about eighteen inches wide, for they traveled single file just as the animals did. They liked to make their paths along high ground where it was usually dry and there was little underbrush and few streams to cross.

Early settlers became well acquainted with these Indian trails, and called them by such names as *Indian path, Indian road, Indian trace, Indian trading path, Indian trail.* Sometimes they called them *warriors' paths,* especially if they were often used by warriors invading each other's territories.

The longest and most important of these old warriors'

paths was one used by the northern and the southern Indians in their wars on each other in the general area of what is now Kentucky. This beautiful region was their no man's land, where bloodshed and strife were the order of the day.

This path began not far from the present city of Chattanooga, Tennessee. It wound north through the Blue Ridge Mountains, which it left at Cumberland Gap. From there it made straight for the Ohio River which it crossed at the mouth of the Scioto. Then it continued to Lake Erie and the Indian settlements there. This warriors' path was at least five hundred miles long. At various places it was joined by other paths from the east and west.

WHIP-POOR-WILL   Birds are not able to talk well enough to carry on conversations with people, but many of them utter notes that can easily be put into words. One well-known but seldom seen bird has a grudge against a poor fellow named Will. He shouts to everybody in hearing that Will should be soundly thrashed. He says "Whip-poor-will" over and over again, and seems determined to get the poor man in trouble. Nobody knows just who Will is or why he should be whipped. One bird-lover thought he would count the number of times this bird called out this phrase. He wrote:

> "This bird actually laid upon the back of poor Will one thousand and eighty-eight blows, with only a barely perceptible pause here and there, as if to catch its breath. Then it stopped about half a minute and began again,

uttering this time three hundred and ninety calls, when it paused, flew a little further away, took up the tale once more and continued till I fell asleep."

This bird has a cousin who is also interested in Will but in an indirect way. He asks everybody to *chuck-will's-widow*. That is, he wants everybody to give Will's widow a light tap or pat under the chin. He must know the widow, and feel sure that act of familiarity will not offend her.

Some people think he is constantly advising a young man named John to marry the widow. He says over and over *John-marry-the-widow, John-marry-the-widow*. But John is apparently a shy fellow, or maybe he thinks he does not have much chance with the widow. Whether he is even engaged to her nobody knows.

Still others think this bird is saying that a chip fell out of the white oak. He certainly seems to say *chip-fell-out-of-the-white-oak*. This could be the beginning of a very good story, but what is the rest of it? Why did the chip fall out, and what happened then?

WILDERNESS ROAD or TRAIL   Pioneers would not be pioneers if they weren't willing to face adventure and change. As soon as settlements became fairly numerous east of the Blue Ridge Mountains, adventurous hunters like Daniel Boone ventured farther and farther west in search of more fertile lands where game was plentiful.

Before the Revolution, some of these bold woodsmen

had crossed the mountains and found that what is now the State of Kentucky was a garden of Eden. They went home and spread the news about the good land beyond the mountains. Boone and about thirty of his friends set out from the Watauga Settlements in what is now the eastern part of Tennessee, making a road to the new lands as best they could.

They threaded their way down the valleys and across the mountains until they reached Cumberland Gap. Then they turned northwest to the mouth of Otter Creek on the Kentucky River in the heart of the new land. They later built a fort here and called it Boonesboro.

Soon this way, or trail, was being used by pioneers toiling over the mountains to settle in the new country. They encountered hardships that discouraged all but the most resolute. In places the trail was so narrow a wagon could not be driven along it. Streams had to be crossed. It was easy for the Indians to fall upon the pioneers in the dark forest and kill or capture them and all their possessions. They killed more than a hundred in 1784.

But from 1775 to 1825 this old Wilderness Road or Trail as it is now called was used by thousands of frontiersmen determined to settle in Kentucky. And some parts of this old road are still in use to this day, forming part of U.S. Route No. 25, better known as the Dixie Highway.

WINONA   Among the words borrowed in this country from the Indians *Winona* is the only one used as the name for a girl. For some reason *Pocahontas*, a pretty name, has never been fancied by white parents, nor has *Minnehaha,* meaning "Laughing Water," fared any better.

The Dakota Indians, however, gave the name *Winona* to the first girl child born to a couple, and this name is sometimes used by those who are not Indians. The most famous girl of this name was the daughter of Nokomis in Longfellow's *Song of Hiawatha.* The poet says:

> On the Muskoday, the meadow,
> In the moonlight and the starlight,
> Fair Nokomis bore a daughter.
> And she called her name Wenonah,
> As the first-born of her daughters.
> And the daughter of Nokomis
> Grew up like the prairie lilies,
> Grew a tall and slender maiden,
> With the beauty of the moonlight,
> With the beauty of the starlight.

WOODBINE, *gone where the woodbine twineth* Formerly this phrase was often used colloquially of one who had died or gone away to some distant place where he would probably not be heard from again.

The phrase arose in 1870 from a song with this title by Septimus Winner, a popular song writer in his day. The events of the Civil War were fresh in the writer's mind, and he wrote the song as a tribute to those who had perished in the awful conflict. The woodbine is a honey-suckle, and in former times was often planted on graves. The chorus of Winner's song alludes to this use of the plant:

Then go where the woodbine twineth,
When spring is bright and fair,
And to the soldier's resting place
Some little tribute bear.

WOODCHUCK   When the first settlers in Virginia became established in their new homes, they found in the wilderness about them a heavy-bodied, short-tailed brownish animal about twenty to twenty-five inches long and weighing about ten pounds. As they often did, the settlers asked their Indian friends what they called this creature. Pronouncing as best they could the Indian name, the settlers called the creature a *moonack*.

This name did not make much sense to white people, and they soon made it into *moonax*, or *moonox*, words that could be pronounced by anyone. But for some reason this name even with its simplified pronunciation did not become popular.

Traders and hunters in the region of Hudson Bay called this animal a *woodschock*, *woodshaw*, or *wejack*. In fashioning these words the frontiersmen started from an Indian name, but just what that was it is not easy to say. Whatever the Indian name might have been, however, the natives did not use it for the moonack at all but for another animal found in their country, a mammal like the marten that is now known as a *fisher*, or *pekan*.

The frontiersmen, though, were not careful in such matters. They gave the wrong name to the little animal and did the best they could with the pronunciation of the word they had added to the language. It was not long until those who found it troublesome to say *woodschock* reduced it to *woodchuck*. This name is entirely satisfactory. It can be easily pronounced, and it has an English look about it which *woodschock* lacks. *Woodchuck* pleased everybody.

But *woodchuck* is a puzzling term for those who do not know how it came about. Its parts, *wood* and *chuck,* are common words; but in the expression neither of them has the slightest reference to its usual meaning.

The name has given rise to a jingle that is not easy to say rapidly: "How much wood would a woodchuck chuck if a woodchuck would chuck wood?"

The answer is: "A woodchuck would chuck all the wood a woodchuck would, if a woodchuck would chuck wood."

YANKEE   It would be hard to find a word that has been more diligently studied than this one. Unfortunately very little has been found out about its origin.

Some students are inclined to think it may be the Dutch word *Jan,* the name for John, with a diminutive -*ee* at the end, somewhat as *cookee,* usually spelled *cookie, cooky,* is a diminutive of *koek,* "cake." It seems certain that the word did not originate in this country, for "Yankey Dutch," and other examples of the term, have been found in British use as early as 1683.

But it was on this side of the ocean that the word was first applied as a scornful nickname to some New England frontiersmen serving in the army of General James Wolfe in the French and Indian War. The general did not have the slightest respect for these backwoodsmen.

They were not disciplined. They had no thought of standing up in an open place and being shot down like well-trained European soldiers would. They got behind trees and rocks and fought as the Indians did. General Wolfe and his soldiers thought this was cowardly. And when they cared to, these fellows left the army and went home.

So in 1758 General Wolfe referred to them in far from complimentary terms as "Yankees." Where he got the expression nobody knows. Probably it was a slang term that had sprung up among the British soldiers as a term of contempt for the frontiersmen who pretended to be soldiers with them. The nickname proved popular and was soon much in favor with those who did not care much for the New Englanders.

A term of scorn and disdain sometimes develops into an expression of honor and pride. This change took place in *Yankee*. The tide began to turn in its favor on April 19, 1775. On that date some British soldiers marched out of Boston to destroy some military stores the Americans had at Concord, twenty-two miles away. The patriots learned about the expedition by the time it started, and the whole countryside along the route swarmed with enraged citizens armed with such guns and clubs as they could get.

Before the day was over, these undisciplined Americans had prevented the British soldiers from destroying much of their supplies and had killed and wounded about three hundred of them. No wonder these "country bumpkins," as the soldiers regarded them, were proud of their success. For the first time they now began to call themselves "Yankees," and to take pride in their new name. They also took up the catchy tune "Yankee Doodle," which their enemies had been fond of playing in scorn of them; and from then on the Americans dinned it into the ears of the redcoats until these soldiers were sick and tired of it.

Besides advancing in dignity, *Yankee* became more widely applied. Now it is often used by people abroad as a name for Americans in general, but here at home it is still restricted to New Englanders and those of the Northern states.

YOSEMITE   This name is one of exceptional beauty and usefulness. It occurs in *Yosemite Falls, Yosemite National Park, Yosemite Valley, Yosemite Incline, Yosemite Lake.*

It was used first of the wonderful valley which it designates. As late as the middle of the nineteenth century this spot was the home and hideaway of Indians who were noted killers and thieves. From their place of security in the valley where they thought they were safe from pursuit, they slipped out and murdered and robbed other Indians in that area. When white people came into the region to search for gold, carry on trading operations, and to start ranches these Indians made raids on them.

California officials took prompt notice of these outbreaks, and early in 1851 sent an armed force of about two hundred men against the marauders. In March, this force entered the now famous valley, and as the soldiers sat around their first campfire in the hitherto almost unknown wonderland the question of a name for the place came up for discussion.

L. H. Bunnell proposed to his fellow members of the battalion that they name the place Yo-sem-i-ty—after the Indians they were pursuing. This name, Bunnell stated, was the Indian word for a full-grown grizzly bear. It is now agreed that he was correct in his understanding of the name he suggested. The word appears to come from an Indian term meaning literally, "the killers," and was used by the natives in that region not only for grizzly bears but also for these valley Indians whose ferocity and cruelness had earned them this name.

At first some of the men objected to preserving the name of these wicked Indians, but after the matter had been thoroughly debated and other names had been considered, *Yosemite*, as it was soon written, won almost unanimously.

YO-YO   About 1790 someone in England or France invented a toy consisting of a small wheel with a groove in it to receive a spring. The thing was so made that when tossed from the hand it would return again. In England it was known as a *quiz*, and in France as a *bandalore*. Scholars have never been able to find out the reasons for these names.

About a hundred years later a toy maker from Chicago was in a Paris museum. He found there a bandalore, and learned of how popular it had once been. He studied the old toy carefully and decided it could be improved and once more interest children.

It was not long until the American had succeeded in making a small wooden toy having its two disk-shaped halves connected by a strong spindle around which a string is fitted loosely. One end of the string is looped around the operator's finger and when the toy is tossed away in a certain manner it goes to the limit of the string and returns.

A name was needed for the improved novelty. Neither *bandalore* nor *quiz* was suitable, for the new toy was not the same as that which had preceded it. One of those interested in securing a name for the toy noticed that in some of their games children often called out to each other "You-You!" By striking out the -*u*'s in this expression "Yo-Yo" was left.

The manufacturer was so pleased with this clever name that he at once registered it as a trade-mark in the United States Patent Office.

ZWIEBACK   Ways of feeding babies and small children vary from one generation to another. You might ask your mother if when you were very small you ate *zwieback*. You might well have done so, for this name for a form of thoroughly baked, well-toasted bread came into American English more than fifty years ago.

It was borrowed from the German, probably in New York City. As an English word *zwieback* looks rather odd.

It appears to be the German word for "two" and the English word "back," but it is not quite that. The second part of it is from the German verb *backen*, "to bake," and the significance of the name is "twice baked." In its make-up, therefore, *zwieback* is quite similar to *biscuit*. This old English term, borrowed from Old French, is made up of two elements, *bis-* and *cuit*, and means, literally, "twice cooked."

List of American Words

air brake, 31-32
American, 32-33
anesthesia, 33-35. *See also* letheon.
Annie Oakley, 35-37
Appaloosa horse, 37-38
appendicitis, 38-39
Arbor Day, 39
ax, to have an ax to grind, 39-41

baking powder, 41-42
bald eagle, 42-44
ball, to be behind the eight ball, 44
bathysphere, 44-45
bay lynx, 46
bee, 47
belittle, 47-48
Belshnickle. *See* Santa Claus.

big tree, 194
black widow, 48-49
bobcat, bob-tailed cat, 46
bobolink, 49-50
boll weevil, 50-51
bond paper, 51-52
boss, 52-53
Bowery, 53
brain trust, 53-54
bristlecone pine, 54-55
Broadway, 55-56
Bronx, 57
buckeye, 57-58

cablegram, 58-59
calliope, 59
calumet, 60-61
canoe birch, 61-62
Capitol, 62-63
carrousel, 63

241

ABOUT THE AUTHOR

MITFORD M. MATHEWS, formerly Professorial Lecturer in the Department of Linguistics at the University of Chicago, has been interested in American lexicography for more than thirty years. An amiable Alabama-born scholar, Dr. Mathews was a member of the first lexicography class taught at the University of Chicago in 1925 by the distinguished British scholar Sir William Craigie. For nineteen years he worked with Sir William editing *A Dictionary of American English*.

Dr. Mathew's enthusiasm for words and the often fascinating detective work necessary to trace their origins has resulted in many books on the subject, including *Beginnings of American English, Survey of English Dictionaries, Sources of Southernisms, Dictionary of Americanisms*, and *Words: How To Know Them*. His latest book, *American Words*, was written to acquaint the young reader with some of the many words and phrases that through the years have added to and enriched the English language in the United States.